RESILIENT LEADERSHIP 2.0

REVISED AND EXPANDED EDITION

RESILIENT LEADERSHIP 2.0

REVISED AND EXPANDED EDITION

LEADING WITH CALM, CLARITY,
AND CONVICTION IN ANXIOUS TIMES

Bob Duggan and Bridgette Theurer

Printed in the United States of America
Second Edition

ISBN: 9798322804918

ACKNOWLEDGMENTS TO THE FIRST EDITION

The image of standing on the shoulders of a giant is often used by authors or speakers who appreciate how indebted they are to those who have gone before them. We feel like a better image for us might be that we are perched on the top of a totem pole, supported by a stack of faces representing the many, many people who have enriched our understanding of what it takes to be a truly great leader.

The foundation of that pillar of contributors is Murray Bowen, whose natural systems theory continues to inspire researchers and thinkers across a broad spectrum of the human sciences. One of his disciples, Ed Friedman, recognized the power of Bowen's framework and used it to elaborate an entirely new understanding of leadership. In its own way, Ed's genius was every bit as provocative and creative as that of his mentor, and we have had the privilege of using his work as a major "source code" for the Resilient Leadership model—something Bob Duggan and Jim Moyer acknowledged in their 2009 book by the same name.

In the ten years since Jim and Bob started working on that book, the three of us—Jim, Bob, and Bridgette—have continued to collaborate closely, refining and further evolving the RL model, elaborating on seminal ideas from the book, experimenting with how best to convey practical applications of key ideas, and always searching for language and tools that would make the content of the RL model more accessible to clients in a wide range of business environments. That process of maturing our thoughts about leadership and growing our skills at communicating them to others has been possible because of many hundreds of additional faces on the totem pole. All along the way, the clients to whom we have provided coaching, training, and consulting services have enriched our thinking with their questions, their challenges, and their insightful feedback about the lived practice of Resilient Leadership day in, and day out. We hope their many stories included in this book will give you a feel for the countless ways they have contributed to the wisdom in its pages.

Our names are on the cover of this book, but right at the top of the totem pole with us is Jim Moyer, our partner in Resilient Leadership LLC, whose enthusiasm and boundless energy continues to push us regularly to expand our reach and deepen our thinking. Finally, as every author knows, writing a book is never possible without the support of family, and both of us have been the beneficiaries of family members whose encouragement has been given abundantly and generously. To every single face on that totem pole, we are deeply indebted and profoundly grateful.

Bob Duggan and Bridgette Theurer

ACKNOWLEDGMENTS TO THE SECOND EDITION

A special thank you and debt of gratitude is owed to Doug Theurer, for doing the heavy lifting of reviewing the original manuscript, compiling, re-formatting, and proofreading the second edition, and bringing his attention to detail in every facet of publishing this book, including helping with the design of the new cover. Without his tireless efforts, there would not be a second edition!

We want to extend our appreciation to our certified Resilient Leadership Coaches and Trainers (too many to name here but you know who you are), who so expertly and enthusiastically share their knowledge of Resilient Leadership with their communities and clients.

A shout-out to Irvine Nugent, Bridgette's partner in The Resilient Leadership Podcast, who brings his passion, energy, and insight to our discussions about how leaders can be more resilient in a VUCA world.

And lastly, thank you to our good friend and colleague Jim Moyer, who along with his partner in RL LLC, Jim Burns, continues to expand the reach and impact of Resilient Leadership far and wide.

Bob Duggan and Bridgette Theurer

CONTENTS

INTRODUCTION TO THE FIRST EDITION

More than ten years ago, Bob Duggan, Bridgette Theurer, and Jim Moyer began sharing with one another their conviction that the groundbreaking work of Murray Bowen and Edwin Friedman on Emotional Systems needed to be more widely available to the kinds of clients that each of them regularly dealt with in their consulting and coaching practices. Out of a number of collaborative engagements and many hours of brainstorming and planning together, the three of them agreed on the rough outlines of a model of leadership that they felt captured the theoretical work of Bowen and Friedman yet served the practical needs of leaders in government, the nonprofit sector, and corporate America.

Jim and Bob put together the Resilient Leadership model in a book by the same name, published in 2009. Since that time, the team has continued to evolve and refine the model, thanks to the hundreds of clients who have offered feedback on the Resilient Leadership training and coaching they have received individually and as part of organization-wide engagements. Now, Bob and Bridgette have written this new book to share with leaders everywhere the further evolution of the Resilient Leadership model and the many practical tools for leaders that we have developed since the model's introduction nearly ten years ago.

To appreciate the content of this work, it is not essential to have read our previous book, although we encourage you to do so at some point. For those who have read *Resilient Leadership* or participated in one of our training and / or coaching engagements, there will be many familiar ideas in the pages that follow, but you will quickly see that this book is not a rehash of original material. Rather, in every chapter there are new ideas and new ways of expressing familiar ideas.

In our previous book, we told a single story of an individual who learned to become a more resilient leader. The story was fictional, but it was built out of many real-life experiences from actual clients. In this book, you will find many more stories—brief illustrations of each idea—and all of them were true, real-life client situations. However, we have changed all names and identifying details to ensure the confidentiality we promise all of our clients.

We have tried to structure this book to allow you to skip around from chapter to chapter according to your areas of interest. If there are no particular ideas you want to read about before others, then it will be most helpful for you to read from beginning to end. We also summarize key ideas at the end of each chapter, so you can get a quick overview of the entire book by reading through those first, and then you can go back to dig more deeply by reading the 3 Big Ideas and the stories that flesh them out.

At the end of each chapter, we offer two Core Practices as a means of integrating the concepts and applying them to your daily routine. These Core Practices have been field-tested by our clients and have been shown to be valuable in bridging the gap between insight and practical application.

Our Appendix includes a number of tools—some that we have developed for our various training programs over the years, and some that are new. Along with the Core Practices, we hope that these will be another resource to help you apply Resilient Leadership to your work and life.

We believe deeply that the development of more resilient leaders can change families, teams, organizations, and the world for the better. We hope this book contributes to your development as a more resilient leader, and, in doing so, improves your world.

INTRODUCTION TO THE SECOND EDITION

When we were working on the manuscript for *Resilient Leadership 2.0* in 2015-16, we recognized the extent to which contemporary leaders are dealing on an almost daily basis with the challenges of a VUCA world—one characterized by Volatility, Uncertainty, Complexity, and Ambiguity. Our hope was to provide both emerging and seasoned leaders at every level with practical, accessible help that was faithful to our source code, yet suitable for addressing the many challenging situations that neither Bowen nor Friedman could have foreseen with any degree of specificity from their 20th century vantage points. The feedback we have received to date from our readers has reassured us that our efforts have been on target and have met with a measure of success.

In the decade that has transpired since we first began to discuss writing *Resilient Leadership 2.0*, the pace of change has accelerated and the VUCA world has gotten increasingly volatile, uncertain, complex, and ambiguous. Leaders have had to deal with a pandemic that upended virtually every aspect of their workplace, their strategic plans, their mission, and the available resources they once counted on to manage foreseeable challenges. The global economy has been more unpredictable than ever. The once unthinkable prospect of another horrific war on European soil has become a terrifying reality and long-standing hostilities in the Middle East have once again resulted in unspeakable violence. Competition between democracy and autocracy has spawned struggles whose dimensions have dramatically reshaped the geopolitical landscape around the globe. Even the savviest experts have been stunned at how rapidly the advent of AI has transformed the world of technology, with some warning of an apocalyptic outcome while others foresee unimaginable progress characterizing our human condition. And did we mention the impact of climate change…? The twenty-first century is proving to be a VUCA world on steroids!

The appearance of this second edition of *Resilient Leadership 2.0* reflects our commitment to continue to evolve the RL model to match the escalating challenges of a world that is deeply entrenched in regressive patterns that are challenging even the most seasoned of leaders. The bulk of the material in our original edition of this book has withstood the test of time and continues to help leaders grow in their ability to be better-differentiated leaders—at home, and at work. We have enriched the book's offerings by adding three new chapters:

Chapter 9: Curiosity, which takes a deeper dive into this leadership superpower and explores how curiosity can transform teams, organizations, and even families, helping them to be more resilient in the face of a VUCA world.
Chapter 10: The Neuroscience of Resilient Leadership, which delves into the growing and rapidly developing resources of neuroscience that are helping to support, refine, and deepen the Resilient Leadership model.
Chapter 11: Putting It All Together, which explores how leaders can embody all three of the dimensions of Resilient Leadership (Stay Calm, Stay the Course, and Stay Connected) in a balanced and fluid way, and the benefits that accrue to them when they do.

We have also added a new appendix with additional tools to help leaders apply the principles of resilient leadership in their daily lives. Of particular note is the "Leadership Default Styles" self-assessment on page 262 and the "How to Tame Your Triggers" worksheet on page 258. Both help leaders become more aware of (and less vulnerable to) the patterns of behavior they default to when under pressure and duress, which often interfere with their ability to realize their own potential and the potential of those they lead.

We firmly believe, as did Edwin Friedman, that the emergence of better-differentiated leaders who can withstand the headwinds of resistance and sabotage is what will calm our anxious organizations, families, and world. Such leaders are made, not born. We believe that the kind of leadership development efforts embodied in Resilient Leadership can go a long way towards developing such leadership at all levels, and in all those who are brave enough to lead during these tumultuous times.

CHAPTER 1

RESILIENT LEADERSHIP
A NEW WAY OF SEEING, THINKING, LEADING

All truths are easy to understand once they are discovered;
the point is to discover them.

—*Galileo Galilei*

Resilient Leadership is a new way of SEEING, THINKING, and LEADING that helps leaders navigate the hidden dynamics of organizations more effectively.

Resilient Leaders are able to:

- **Lead with calm, clarity, and conviction in the midst of anxiety provoked by increasing complexity and accelerating change.**
- **Lead from strength. They know how to care for themselves emotionally, spiritually, and physically and can sustain their leadership efforts over time.**

In his best-selling book The 7 Habits of Highly Effective People, *Stephen R. Covey illustrates the power of a "paradigm shift" by quoting a humorous story about the captain on the bridge of a battleship on a dark, foggy night who saw a light that appeared to be coming straight at his ship. The captain ordered his signalman to tell the approaching ship to change course. Its immediate response was something to the effect of, "No, you change course." The captain barked at his signalman to message, "I am the captain, and we are a battleship.* CHANGE COURSE!" *The signalman replied, "I am a seaman second class, and we are a lighthouse. Change course!"*

The story is delightfully humorous and reportedly true. It drives home the power of a paradigm shift that provokes a new way of seeing, which in turn brings with it a whole new way of understanding and thinking and, inevitably, a new way of acting.

Galileo Galilei showed the enormous potential of a new way of seeing. While widely criticized in his day, Galileo's discovery of a Sun-centered universe upset old paradigms, opened the door to questioning established beliefs, and paved the way for a universe far grander than previously imagined. It marked a turning point in science, where observation and evidence became paramount. As a consequence, Galileo was able to lead others to a new understanding that shattered what Edwin Friedman called the "imaginative gridlock" of an entire civilization. That is the power of a paradigm shift!

Paradigm Shift

We believe that Resilient Leadership represents a paradigm shift in how leaders can see, think, and lead in new ways—ways that are distinctively different from traditional models of leadership. Thomas Kuhn, who researched how scientific breakthroughs occur, introduced the term "paradigm shift" into our popular vocabulary. He helped us understand that although it may sometimes seem like a sudden event, the "sudden awakening" of a paradigm shift actually follows a gradual accumulation of information and data from research and experiments, an increasing body of insights into what "works" and what no longer works, and a growing consensus that finally reaches a tipping point that can seem as if a brand-new discovery has "suddenly" been made.

Murray Bowen started thinking in new ways in the 1950s about how to treat his psychiatric patients—no longer as isolated individuals but as members of a family system—and over the next forty years, he deepened his understanding of how emotional systems operate. Edwin Friedman, a Bowen disciple, wrote his first major book on leadership (*Generation to Generation*) from the perspective of Bowen's theory in the early 1980s, and he said at that time that he had been developing his new way of thinking about leadership for a quarter of a century.

We did a simple Google search on *leadership* recently, and in less than two seconds, "about 774,000,000 results" were reported. Clearly, lots of people are thinking about, researching, writing about, and searching for answers about "leadership" these days, so it may appear a bit presumptuous for us to assert that the Resilient Leadership model is part of a genuine paradigm shift. We are convinced, however, that in the Resilient Leadership model, there is something fresh, something not generally taught in courses about leadership or commonly shared as "the wisdom of experience" by senior leaders who are mentoring new generations of leaders.

Our conviction, after many decades of combined experience in coaching and training both seasoned and rising leaders, is that the twenty-first century truly is experiencing a paradigm shift in understanding and practicing the art of leadership, and the Resilient Leadership model represents the cutting edge of that "awakening." We are confident that this is not just the latest, fad, here today and gone tomorrow. Our confidence is bolstered by how often we have seen that what we share in coaching and training Resilient Leadership resonates with research-based insights from and connections being made in such diverse disciplines as neuroscience, genetics and epigenetics, evolutionary biology, mindfulness, social and positive psychology, emotional intelligence, and more.

Data from those disciplines support much of what we teach, but we are convinced that the insights of Resilient Leadership operate on a deeper level of inquiry. We have tried to capture the essence of the Resilient Leadership model's breakthrough perspective by describing a New Way of SEEING, THINKING, and LEADING. We will come back to all three of these dimensions of leadership in each of the chapters that follow; here, however, we want to give a high-level overview of the unique perspective that each dimension offers.

A New Way of SEEING: Observe the Emotional System

We were working with a senior leadership team in a large Washington, DC, law firm, and when we introduced the notion that leaders should pay attention to the emotional system of their organization, a very brilliant senior partner strongly objected. "I leave my emotions at home," he said, "and I expect everyone on my staff to do the same. This is a professional organization, and emotions have no place in it!" We pushed back—gently, we thought—and he became even more animated. "I'm sick and tired of this touchy-feely stuff we hear from consultants like you. We've earned the success we've enjoyed over the years because our people bring an objective mindset to the business of the law, and we don't let emotions get in the way of doing business." The intensity with which he spoke, the pink flush on his face, and the throbbing vein in his neck told us it was not a good idea to argue our case at that moment. But we were fairly certain that everyone else in the room was keenly aware that the senior leader had just provided quite a display of a reactive emotional system.

One of the core tenets of the Resilient Leadership model is that every organization, every family—in fact, every network of relationships at any scale—is composed of both a **rational system** and an **emotional system**, and these are constantly interacting with each other. The rational system includes all of the facts and figures that every leader has been trained to pay attention to and to manage: P&L statements, three-to-five-year performance-to-plan growth targets, organizational charts, roles, responsibilities, work processes, project-management technology, agendas, deliverables, employee-engagement statistics, customer-satisfaction numbers, and a long, long list of other items that leaders are most often accountable to manage. The rational system is observable and is made up of objective information and data that can be measured, studied, manipulated, reengineered, rightsized, and so forth.

Understanding the Emotional System

The emotional system is the other half of the story, and we believe that it is an even bigger driver of performance and results. We define the emotional system as the instinctive pattern of automatic actions, reactions, and interactions that shape the functioning of an individual, team, organization, or any network of relationships.

> **The emotional system is comprised of the instinctive pattern of automatic actions, reactions and interactions that shape the functioning of an individual, team, or organization.**

Think of an emotional system as an invisible force field—almost all of which lies beneath conscious awareness—that binds the members of a system together and becomes stronger and more firmly entrenched the longer those members work or live together. We refer to the emotional system as the "hidden chemistry" of organizations. But what are the elements that characterize that chemistry? Perhaps the easiest way to understand how the emotional system works in an organization is to reflect on how it works within each of us as individuals since every person has both a rational part of her/his makeup and an emotional part: a thinking self and a feeling self.

Our favorite graphic to help leaders understand the emotional system is the picture of an iceberg, where the visible part is the smallest—the rational system—while hidden below the water (beneath conscious awareness) is the larger, more formidable part. As you look at the graphic, you'll notice that down at the deepest level, we signal the presence of instinctual, primal forces. We are suggesting that deep below our conscious awareness is a life force that drives every living being to remain in existence, to survive "at all costs." As a result, we humans have evolved a brain that is constantly on the alert for threats.

Chronic Anxiety

Murray Bowen gave a name to this energy—this life force—that is constantly swirling beneath our conscious awareness: **chronic anxiety**. Our definition of chronic anxiety is "an abiding sense of unease about imagined or anticipated threats." The key word here is "abiding," never absent, because anxiety is, quite literally, essential for our survival. Chronic anxiety is like the air we breathe. It is around us and within us, and we depend on it for continued life, but we can never "see" it directly. Depending on many factors, such as the history of our ancestors and the environment into which we are born, we grow up with a lower or higher level of chronic anxiety. Too little chronic anxiety puts us at risk of not dealing with real threats; too much cripples us with an excessive preoccupation over basic survival. Just the right amount results in a healthy individual who knows how to lead a "balanced" life.

The emotional system of a person or an organization is the key to healthy functioning and success in the world. That is why we insist that learning to "observe the emotional system" is the essential first step to becoming a resilient leader. Not surprisingly (since every organization is made up of people), too little chronic anxiety within the emotional system of an organization makes it complacent and puts it at risk of being overtaken by competitors; too much anxiety makes it overly risk averse, and it will fail to grow and evolve to stay even with or ahead of the competition. Either of these options can cause a fatal breakdown in the organization's performance, while "just the right amount" of chronic anxiety usually spells success. Resilient

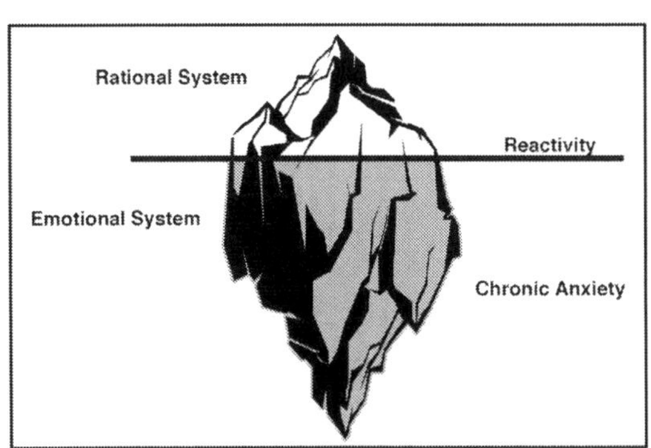

Leadership suggests that it is the role of an organization's leader to continually monitor the ebb and flow of anxiety and to use the right tools to maintain a healthy balance that spells organizational success.

But you may be asking yourself, "How is a leader supposed to monitor something (like chronic anxiety) that is invisible to the naked eye and beneath conscious awareness?" Going back to the iceberg graphic, you'll see that breaking through the waterline is "Reactivity," which we call the "public face of anxiety." The resilient leader is one who has learned to watch for subtle (and sometimes not-so-subtle) signs of reactivity in her/himself—and in the organization s/he leads.

Reactivity

On the individual level, here are some signals of reactivity that can alert us that we are carrying an unhealthy level of anxiety: a racing mind, tension in the neck and shoulders, a knot in the stomach, restless sleep or inability to sleep, or difficulty staying focused. There are myriad other ways that escalating chronic anxiety makes itself felt and known in every dimension of our lives. On the organizational level, there are similar signs of deficit or excess that can alert a leader to the need to raise urgency or dial down anxiety. We deal with these in some detail in the next chapter and also in the chapters on Triangles and Over/Underfunctioning, both of which are visible expressions of anxiety. But the point to note here is the importance of learning about reactivity—the positive, healthy kind that keeps us alive and flourishing, as well as the hyperreactivity that can do us in.

Recognizing reactivity and how it works, and being a more astute observer of the emotional system (in self, others, or an entire organization)—like any other skill—can be developed over time and with practice. A guide, mentor, or coach can help point out what to look for, but ultimately, it is the leader's commitment to and patience with the gradual nature of mastering this New Way of SEEING that is required to develop proficiency in this key leadership competency.

Getting On the Balcony

One of the most powerful practices we know of that can help us develop this skill is called "getting on the balcony" (an image popularized by Ronald Heifetz in his book *Leadership on the Line*). The image is that of a crowded ballroom full of dancers, with a balcony at one end. As you are dancing with your partner, you mentally put yourself up on the balcony and observe how you are interacting with him/her. But from the balcony, you can observe not only yourself but also how your partner and others in the room are dancing. Finally, from that same vantage point, you can simultaneously follow the overall movement and flow of all of the dancers in the room as they sway and move to the rhythm and beat of the music.

In the context of the Resilient Leadership model, to "get on the balcony" means to observe the emotional system by observing the flow of reactive, instinctual, automatic functioning—in yourself, in others, and in the system at large. As you develop some level of proficiency in this skill, you will be able to observe with a more detached curiosity, which will immediately lower your reactivity and make you more thoughtful. A mindset of curiosity always makes a person more thoughtful and, as a consequence, less reactive. As a practice that can help you manage your chronic anxiety more skillfully, getting on the balcony is as good as it gets.

STOP & REFLECT

- **Chronic anxiety is an "abiding state of unease in the face of imagined or anticipated threats." What imagined or anticipated threats (e.g., threats to your safety or that of your loved ones, security in your position at work, etc.) might be fueling your current level of chronic anxiety?**
- **Our bodies often reveal the presence of chronic anxiety before we are consciously aware of it. How does chronic anxiety manifest itself in your body—for example, a knot in your stomach, clenched jaw, or tension in your neck or shoulders?**

A New Way of THINKING: Think Systems

Marvin, the CEO of a midsize manufacturing company, was experiencing a growing problem with quality control, even though the company had been ISO 9001 certified for many years and was well regarded in the industry for the dependability of its products. The company supplied highly specialized parts for the aerospace industry, and Marvin knew well that if his quality issues were not soon resolved, orders would be canceled and the very existence of the company might be at risk. He had done everything humanly possible to verify that the QC system exceeded industry standards, but problems persisted. Absenteeism and work-related injuries had been growing steadily for more than a year; separate divisions that previously had collaborated smoothly were blaming each other for breakdowns; and even some of his most trusted, longtime managers were starting to talk about early retirement because of the bickering and infighting they had to deal with every day. He was out of solutions to try.

Another CEO who had recently worked with us recommended that Marvin, a friend of his, give us a call. Mostly out of desperation, Marvin did so and asked us to help him understand what was the source of the inexplicable surge in QC problems now threatening the solid family business that his father had built. At the risk of offering too brief a summary of our twelve-month engagement, here is what we found as we tried to help Marvin and his leadership team observe the emotional system and the think systems:

- There was no evidence that the problems came from any flaws in the rational system. All of the QC policies and procedures in place were sound and had been functioning well for many years.
- The emotional system, however, was in chaos, and anxiety had been escalating in the company for several years in ways and for reasons that (in retrospect) were very obvious.

These are some of the factors that we discovered were contributing to the turmoil in the company's emotional system:

- Marvin's father, who had founded, built, and run the company for nearly forty years, had died suddenly about three years earlier. There had been no formal succession plan to replace him, but Marvin was the oldest son and had been with the company for more than ten years, so he'd stepped into the leadership role.
- Within several months, Marvin began implementing significant changes that he had lobbied his reluctant father to consider for many years.

- Although neither of Marvin's two younger brothers wanted or was equipped to run the company, as co-owners, they second-guessed many of Marvin's decisions and had even outvoted him twice on some expansion plans he felt were important for the company's future.
- Tensions between Marvin and his brothers were growing, and despite efforts to keep their differences among themselves, a number of the senior leaders had figured out that there was trouble brewing.
- Marvin's father had been an extrovert, believed in "management by walking around," and knew nearly all of the employees by first name. Marvin was a strong introvert, needed space and quiet, and felt most comfortable communicating with his employees through technology.
- Shortly after his father's death, Marvin had gotten wind that unionization efforts were afoot, and he'd brought in an aggressive group of "union busters" to help him "wage war" on the organizers. The outcome was still uncertain.

Any one of these factors would have raised the anxiety level of a previously stable organization, but together, they had seriously destabilized the emotional system built by Marvin's father over many years of steady leadership. Marvin, we discovered, had a fairly limited capacity to observe or understand the kind of nonlinear, interactive processes that characterize relationship systems. For him, to "think systems" meant to engage in a very linear, rational analysis of the mechanical and easily objectified elements that made up the company's rational system.

A leader "thinks systems" by reflecting thoughtfully on the actions, reactions, and interactions s/he has observed.

In addition, Marvin had a fairly low level of self-awareness, which made him oblivious to how much anxiety he was carrying and communicating to those around him as the shocks to the emotional system we enumerated above piled one on top of the other. For his part, Marvin was gradually becoming more and more reactive, and the decisions he was making were less and less thoughtful. Because of his limited ability to "think systems"—especially on the emotional level—the organization he was leading was becoming more and more anxious, more and more reactive. Relationships within the company were becoming stressed and beginning to unravel, and as a result, the rational system was becoming symptomatic, with "inexplicable" declines in productivity, efficiency, and quality.

A leader "thinks systems" by reflecting thoughtfully on the actions, reactions, and interactions s/he has observed among people within the emotional system of which s/he is a part. To get a sense of the extent to which you "think systems" in your role as a leader, see page 245 in the Appendix ("Are You a Systems Thinker?").

In thinking systems, the leader seeks to understand more deeply:

- how interactions have contributed to repetitive patterns, some of which promote healthy functioning while others do not
- how the patterns all fit together to raise or lower anxiety/reactivity within the system
- how s/he needs to adjust his/her functioning to help calm the system and make it more resilient

An Alternative Scenario

How might things have been different if Marvin had been a resilient leader who knew how to observe the emotional system and to think systems? Here is an alternative script that could well have been possible:

- Upon his father's sudden death, Marvin could have recognized its impact on him, his family, and every one of the company's employees and stakeholders. He could have faced and dealt with his feelings of loss and recognized that his entire family system needed time to mourn and draw closer together as a result of shared grief and mutual support. Family bonds could have been strengthened.

- Marvin could also have correctly recognized the shock felt by everyone connected with the company—employees and stakeholders alike. As he took over leadership, a high priority of his first six to twelve months could have been to connect with employees and stakeholders, building bonds of trust and reassuring them of continuity with the company's successful past. He could have been very slow to make any changes that were not absolutely necessary. His staying connected and repeated reassurances could have helped lower anxiety over the implications for the company of the sudden loss of its longtime leader.
- Building a new relationship with his two brothers could have avoided potential conflicts. While working on rational-system issues, he could have also been attentive to the emotional system and paid attention to his brothers' sensitivities as he stepped in to replace their beloved father in the business. He could have acknowledged their equal ownership and worked to clarify his role as CEO and the boundaries of their involvement in decisions regarding the running of the company.
- When he heard of the efforts to unionize, he could have managed his own reactivity and looked for a less confrontational way to neutralize interest in that option. Focusing on getting to know his employees' names, for example, would have been an excellent investment of his time and energy, despite the stretch it would have required of him as an introvert.
- When reactive behaviors surfaced, he could have been intentional about thinking systems, and that would have helped him to recognize those behaviors as symptoms of the predictable anxiety of a system undergoing significant

change. Instead of attacking the symptoms as if they were the problem, he could have first focused on managing his own anxiety and then developed strategies aimed at lowering the anxiety of the system at large.

These examples show how differently Marvin might have handled his role as a new leader. Hopefully, they also show how different the outcomes might have been had Marvin been a resilient leader who knew how to observe the emotional system and then could think systems and formulate a less reactive response. We did not fault Marvin for his shortcomings. We found him to be a very bright, committed leader who cared deeply about the legacy he had inherited from his father. He had an MBA from a prestigious East Coast business school, but even with this top-quality rational-system education, he had not been afforded the opportunity to learn about the power of an organization's emotional system; nor had he been shown the real meaning of thinking systems in that context. For him, to "think systems" meant to focus on all of the moving parts of the rational system and how they needed to interact in order for the business to run smoothly.

STOP & REFLECT

- **Consider for a moment how the emotional system of your team/organization is currently functioning. Is anxiety (and the corresponding level of reactivity) high, low, or somewhere in between? From a systems perspective, what might be contributing to what you see, whether that is anxious reactivity or thoughtful action?**
- **Consider for a moment how the emotional system of your family is currently functioning. Is anxiety (and the corresponding level of reactivity) high, low, or somewhere in between? From a systems perspective,**

what might be contributing to what you see, whether that is anxious reactivity or thoughtful action?

Nearly always, when we coach or train business leaders, they are able to see how the principles and practices we share with them can be transferred to their personal lives with family and friends. The truth is that a person who becomes a resilient leader shows up as such in whatever system s/he is part of. Resilient Leadership is about *being*, above all, and the *doing* follows naturally in every system where the leader is present. The third dimension of the RL model—a New Way of LEADING—is the inevitable outcome of SEEING and THINKING in new ways, and it is to that we now direct your attention.

A New Way of LEADING: Focus on Differentiation of Self

Several years back, Bridgette responded to a request for coaching from Lowell, a concerned leader of a small start-up company. During her initial meeting with him, Lowell described all of the problems he had been having with his team and how they were just not keeping up with the fast pace of change in their industry. As a result of both the complexity and speed of those changes, they were falling further and further behind their competitors. "If I could get them shaped up, we'd be fine," he said. "But I spend all of my time putting out fires because my team isn't doing its job."

Over the next year of coaching and learning about Resilient Leadership, Lowell gradually became more self-aware and began to recognize many of the ways that he was contributing to the problems of the team. Bridgette knew he had reached a significant turning point one day when she was facilitating a strategic-planning retreat for the team. At the end of the day, Lowell said to the group words to this effect: "I think we've put the worst behind us. Thank you for all you've done to get us to where we are today. And I've got to confess to you that I used to think most of our problems were mostly your fault, but what I've come to realize is that we didn't have a team problem—our problem was me and how I was leading."

What was it, then, that Lowell learned about the New Way of LEADING that enabled him to learn how better to support, not hinder, the performance of his team? For more than a decade, when we have been asked to describe what a resilient leader looks like, part of our answer has always been that such an individual **"leads with calm, clarity, and conviction in the midst of anxiety provoked by increasing complexity and accelerating change."** In addition, resilient leaders have learned how to take care of themselves (emotionally, mentally, and physically) and therefore can sustain their leadership efforts over time. More recently, we often add that a resilient leader is well-equipped to lead in a VUCA world.

A VUCA World

The acronym VUCA ("volatility, uncertainty, complexity, and ambiguity") was first used at the US Army War College to describe the multilateral world that resulted after the Cold War ended. Today, leaders in every sector find it an apt description of the environment in which they operate. We like to think that the scale of leadership challenges today is unique and unprecedented, but the fact is that from the very beginnings of evolutionary history, every form of life on earth has had to face increasingly complex challenges to survive. Survival has inevitably meant developing increasingly complex adaptations to those challenges. Lowell came to realize the complexity that leadership entails, and he was open to learning

Resilient leaders are equipped to lead in a VUCA world.

about new approaches and the personal transformation required of him if he aimed to embody and become a truly more resilient leader.

The dance of life, so to speak, might be characterized as a continuous effort to maintain a stable internal environment in relation to a constantly changing and evolving external world. Whether we consider being leaders in our families, our communities, or our workplaces, learning how to do the dance of life is a lifelong process of discoveries, constant practice, and steady improvement. For example, scientists tell us that even on such a primitive scale, bacterial colonies have receptors that enable them to "read" their environment and move toward a source of nutrition and away from potential toxins. Strategic planners using a SWOT (strengths, weaknesses, opportunities, threats) analysis are following this same instinctive pattern in an attempt to maintain internal integrity in the face of external challenges that threaten organizational survival. At whatever scale of complexity—from a bacterial colony to a global enterprise—the ability to self-regulate and manage external threats are two essential keys to successfully navigating the dance of life.

The suggestion of the Resilient Leadership model that one leads best by focusing on oneself strikes many as counterintuitive. Lowell certainly was skeptical when Bridgette first suggested that he needed to focus less on the functioning of his team and more on his own functioning. Most leadership-training programs encourage leaders to keep their focus on others, whether by tracking employee engagement, boosting productivity through incentives, or developing elaborate human-capital management systems to hold employees accountable for business goals. We do not dismiss the value of such efforts—they are essential, and leaders must continue to attend to such issues. But we are convinced that self-awareness, self-definition, and self-regulation must be top priorities for leaders. As Lowell gradually made this shift, new horizons opened up for him, and he was able to embrace a whole new understanding of how to lead his team more effectively.

Differentiation

The term **differentiation of self** is a bit of jargon we have borrowed from Murray Bowen, whose work has provided so many foundational insights for the Resilient Leadership model. We have retained the phrase—despite some hesitancy about incorporating psychological jargon—because it is such a richly researched notion and is sufficiently nuanced to help leaders meet the complex challenges of a VUCA world. In fact, we believe there is ample evidence for our conviction that the better differentiated a leader is, the greater is that leader's capacity for effective leadership. (See page 244 in the Appendix to get a sense of the contrast between well-differentiated leaders and poorly differentiated ones.) We have tried to capture the essence of what it means for a leader to be well differentiated with three imperatives: Stay Calm, Stay the Course, and Stay Connected. We will explore each of these in the next three chapters, but by way of preview, we can offer a glimpse here of how each imperative fits as an essential aspect of keeping a focus on differentiation of self as the New Way of LEADING:

Stay Calm. Resilient leaders understand that high levels of chronic anxiety militate against an organization's ability to be nimble, innovative, and resilient. They also realize the irreplaceable role they play—by managing their own anxiety—in helping their organization to be less anxious and more thoughtful. We capture these insights with the two slogans, "Be a Less Anxious Presence" and "Act as a Step-Down Transformer." (More on these imperatives in the next chapter.)

Stay the Course. Resilient leaders are clear within themselves about the vision, values, and principles that guide their life course, both personally and professionally. They know that to remain true to themselves, they must sometimes take risks, and they are not afraid to make bold, self-differentiating moves. They also realize the inevitability of the resistance or sabotage those moves will encounter from a reactive system that seeks, naturally, to maintain its status quo. But, though faced with resistance, they remain thoughtful and can distinguish between reactive complaints and productive complaints, listening openly to the latter and ignoring the content of the former. (We address this imperative in detail in chapter 3.)

Stay Connected. Resilient leaders understand that they are able to exert a positive influence on the system they lead only if they are connected to it in a balanced, healthy way. It is the quality, not the quantity, of their connection that matters. Because all of us get anxious at times, resilient leaders have learned to recognize whether their default tendency under stress is to withdraw (cut off) or move overly close (fuse). The key, they know, to showing up with just the right kind of leadership presence is captured in the phrase "close enough to influence yet distant enough to lead." (For more on this imperative, see chapter 4.)

STOP & REFLECT

- **Of the three Resilient Leadership imperatives described above, which one are you the strongest in, and which one do you most want to strengthen at this time?**
- **How might becoming a more resilient leader benefit you, your team, and/or your family?**

Core Practices

Get On the Balcony
Regularly step back (and up) to broaden your perspective about what is going on in the emotional system of your organization, team, or family. Use the image and metaphor of *being on a balcony* to:

1) *Observe reactivity in yourself and others.* At the end of each day, ask, "What reactive behaviors did I see in myself today, and what reactive behaviors did I see in others?
2) *Think systems.* At the end of each day, ask yourself, "What is going on in the larger system(s)—or in me—that might be contributing to the reactivity that I see?"'
3) *Choose a thoughtful response.* Ask yourself, "What is the most responsible thing for me to do?"

For a more detailed outline of this practice see page 272.

Focus On Your Own Functioning
Whenever you are involved in a challenging situation with another person or group and find yourself tempted to judge or blame others, pause and ask yourself, "What's my part in this?"

This question is not aimed at finding fault with yourself; rather, it is a recognition of the reciprocal dynamics that are always present in emotional systems and is a way of exploring with curiosity how you might be contributing to the anxious reactivity that is swirling around you.

Chapter Summary

- Resilient Leadership is not simply a set of ideas, tools, and techniques to employ but rather a fundamentally new way of SEEING, THINKING, and LEADING. As such, it takes intentional and consistent practice to embody.
- All organizations—from families to large corporations—are composed of both a rational system and an emotional system. Most leaders are trained to pay attention to the former and are either totally unaware of or ill-equipped to navigate the latter.
- Chronic anxiety is "an abiding state of unease in the face of imagined or anticipated threats." It is the instinctive life-force that is embedded in the emotional system of every person and every organization. Just enough chronic anxiety keeps us alert and ready to respond to real threats; too much interferes with our capacity to think clearly, diminishes innovation and risk taking, and leads to an escalation of reactivity.
- The emotional system is that part of the iceberg under the water—invisible and beneath conscious awareness, yet powerful in its impact on performance. A resilient leader learns to observe the emotional system by paying attention to reactivity, the public face of anxiety.
- Resilient leaders are able to lead with "calm, clarity, and conviction in the midst of escalating anxiety and increasing complexity." As such, they are equipped to function in a VUCA world (one characterized by velocity, uncertainty, complexity, and ambiguity).
- Thinking Systems is at the heart of the Resilient Leadership model. It requires that we "get on the balcony" to observe the flow of anxiety and reactivity within and around us and then to *think our way through a situation* to determine the most appropriate and productive actions we can take.
- Resilient Leaders focus more on their own functioning than on changing the behaviors or actions of others. They do this by growing their capacity for self-awareness, self-definition, and self-regulation.

CHAPTER 2

BE A STEP-DOWN TRANSFORMER

BRING A CALMING PRESENCE TO ANXIOUS SYSTEMS

A man of calm is like a shady tree.
People who need shelter come to it.

—Toba Beta
Betelgeuse Incident: Insiden Bait Al-Jauza

As the horror of the 9-11 attacks was unfolding—especially after one of the planes struck the Pentagon—federal-government offices throughout the metropolitan Washington, DC, area braced themselves for the possibility that they might well be the target of further, unimaginable attacks. The scope of the attacks was becoming clearer, and anxiety was escalating rapidly in the Emergency Preparedness Office of one agency located not far from the White House. The office director had not yet arrived, and those who were waiting for her later described the mood as one of confusion, indecision, and near panic. Should they order employees to shelter in place, evacuate, or… what?

Within a very short time, the director—we'll call her Marissa—arrived, quickly debriefed with the duty officer, and called her team together to discuss their response. Marissa was a mature, seasoned veteran who was known far and wide for her ability to remain cool under fire. Within minutes, she was able to help her team calm down, focus on the information at hand, lay out several possible responses, and prioritize their immediate next steps.

During a training in the Resilient Leadership model some years later, several members of her team told Bob and Bridgette that Marissa acted as the perfect embodiment of what they now were able to identify as a step-down transformer. *"As soon as she walked in the room," they said, "you could feel everyone breathe a sigh of relief. We knew she'd help us figure out the right moves to make."*

What's Going On Here?

There was something about Marissa's presence in the midst of what we call **acute anxiety** that helped the entire team become less anxious and more thoughtful. Even before she started to speak, give directions, or gather information, every member of her team knew that with her in the room, they would be able to figure out how they should deal with the many unknowns of a still-terrifying

> ***Acute Anxiety*: A transient state of unease in the face of a current threat.**

situation. In fact, Marissa's calm demeanor had a contagious effect, and as they began to settle, everyone started to think more clearly about the challenges they faced. More than a decade later, members of her team were able to recall that it was Marissa's presence, her very *being*—rather than anything she was able to *do or say*—that helped them regain a measure of calm and thoughtfulness.

> ***Chronic Anxiety*: An abiding sense of unease about imagined or anticipated threats.**

You might have wondered while reading this story whether you would have responded with the same degree of calm confidence and reassuring presence that Marissa did. Regardless of how you might have shown up in that particular situation, we believe that any leader, at any level, can learn to be more of what we call a **step-down transformer**. Such leaders bring a calming influence not only to the kind of high-pressure stakes that Marissa faced in a time of acute anxiety but also to the more mundane, everyday stressors and pressures that characterize the level of chronic anxiety in every organization, every family, and every relationship network.

What is a Step-Down Transformer?

It was Ed Friedman who introduced us to the metaphor of a "step-down transformer" to describe a leader's key responsibility when dealing with a chronically anxious system. Electrical transformers are wired to take the electrical energy of the system that passes through them and reduce its voltage. Similarly, a leader who is properly wired (i.e., who embodies a well-defined presence) is able to reduce the system's anxiety. It is always the case that the energy of an emotional system (its chronic anxiety) flows through the leader of that system. And depending on the quality of that leader's presence, the system's anxiety is either raised or lowered. As we'll see later in this chapter, a leader need not be free of all anxiety to lower the level of chronic anxiety in the system. All that is required is that the leader be a less anxious presence than others in the system.

Marissa's story describes a brief period of acute anxiety rather than the system's abiding level of chronic anxiety. A fitting metaphor for what Marissa did on 9-11 might be that she acted as a surge protector, keeping a sudden spike in voltage from destroying a vital part of the network. Once the voltage spike is over, a surge protector returns to its monitoring status, always ready to engage at the next unexpected voltage spike. We tell Marissa's story because, in addition to being a good "surge protector," she was also highly effective at stepping down the ongoing, everyday kind of anxiety that is present, to a greater or lesser extent, in every organization.

Marissa's team had already experienced her calming influence over several years. They had developed a deep trust in her leadership, and as a result, their level of chronic anxiety was well within healthy bounds. That's why she was able to bring them back so quickly from a state of near panic to one of thoughtfulness. It was her presence—how she was wired—that enabled her to bring almost immediate calm to a very anxious team even amid an acute crisis. That is what a step-down transformer does!

STOP & REFLECT

- **To what extent do you operate now as a step-down transformer in your organization—someone who can exert a calming influence not only in acute situations but on daily pressures and stressors as well? (See "Are You a Step-Down Transformer?" on page 238 in the Appendix.)**

- **When you enter an intense meeting of people who have already gathered for some reason, does your presence tend to raise or lower the existing level of anxiety in the room? Does your arrival promote thoughtfulness? How might you know?**

Now that we know what a step-down transformer is, how do we expand our capability to operate as one? In our previous chapter, we said that Resilient Leadership is a new way of SEEING, not simply a new set of techniques. So we begin our journey toward becoming more of a step-down transformer by learning how to spot reactivity—first in ourselves and then in the various systems we are part of.

First Big Idea—A New Way of SEEING: Become a more astute observer of reactivity in self, others, and systems.

Someone Bob coached once confessed to him an embarrassing lapse into reactivity: Joe had come into the office early to prepare for a much-delayed but important team meeting that required every member to be present. At eight-thirty, one of the team e-mailed that he did not think he would be able to make it in for "personal reasons." This was the second time in the last two weeks that this individual had forced the team to reschedule, and Joe "blew his stack" (his words). Angrily, without thinking, Joe fired off a response expressing his frustration, copying everyone on the team. What ensued was a series of longer and longer e-mails between Joe and the team member, played out in front of the entire team. The rest of the team hid out in their offices for the remainder of the day, keenly aware of Joe's bad mood and hoping they could avoid the spotlight of his glare.

Most of us have been on the sending and/or receiving end of long, contentious e-mail chains that raise anxiety and make clear thinking less likely with each hit of the send button. Such behavior is a common example of anxiety-fueled reactivity. As we discussed in chapter 1, we can't directly observe anxiety, but we can observe the reactive behaviors it produces. Joe was honest enough with himself (and Bob) to recognize and name his behavior for what it was—a reactive, thoughtless lapse.

A Deeper Look at Reactivity

We define reactivity as "an automatic response to a perceived threat or reward." The emphasis here is on the word *automatic*. Most neuroscientists would agree that 95 to 99 percent of our day-to-day behavior is the result of instinct and habit rather than intentional choice. Millions of years of evolution have hardwired into our brains a set of automatic functions that help us stay alive and thrive. Researchers have discovered that roughly every seven seconds, our brains scan our environment for threats, and inside them, the amygdala stands ever-ready to react immediately as soon as a perceived threat appears on the horizon. When our primitive ancestors' most severe threats were wild animals, their automatic responses were often lifesaving. Still today, we automatically duck ("without thinking") when an object is hurled at us, or we automatically swerve the steering wheel when a deer jumps in front of our car.

Reactivity, like anxiety, isn't inherently good or bad, but it does come in many different expressions. Research has come a long way since the pioneering work of Walter Cannon in the 1930s described two automatic responses we share with our evolutionary ancestors—flight and fight. Others have further elaborated on the variety of automatic responses, adding "freeze and appease" and, more recently, "tend and befriend." Seeking to uncover the ancient roots of a whole spectrum of reactive emotions, neuroscientist Jaak Panksepp has identified seven distinct regions of the brain in humans and other mammals where there are "affective neural networks" that generate primal emotional responses which in turn lead to reactive behavior patterns.

Science will continue to identify and probe for a deeper understanding of reactive behaviors, where they come from, and how they operate. But what is already clear is that all reactive behaviors are ultimately responses to perceived threats or rewards, and depending on the context, they can have positive or negative consequences for self or others. The "tend and befriend" stress response, for example, can help us not only to survive but to thrive. This instinct is more predominant in females than males but is present to some extent in most mammals and many other animal species. During adverse times, this automatic response urges us to "tend" to the most vulnerable among us (children, friends in trouble, even strangers who are hurting) by extending a helping hand, even if doing so can put our own safety or well-being at risk. The "befriend" part of the response involves reaching out to form close, stable attachments and affiliations with others, which benefits us and strengthens group cohesion at large.

But in the workplace (and in our own families), our automatic reactions often get us into trouble, as when, "without thinking," we blurt out to our boss how we truly feel about his pet project; or, as Joe did, when we fire off an angry e-mail to our team without pausing to calm ourselves and consider the consequences of the message.

We can become more astute observers of our own reactivity by learning about some of our primal needs that, when threatened, are likely to elicit a strong and immediate reactive response. Research has determined that our brains are programmed to respond in a particularly strong way to perceived threats to these primal needs: control, safety, approval, belonging, and certainty. In reflecting with Bob on his lapse, Joe was able to recognize that it was his need for control—and the feeling that he was losing control of an important project—that had pushed him over the edge.

STOP & REFLECT

- **Which of the five primal needs (control, safety, approval, belonging, or certainty) makes you feel most provoked when it is threatened or not being fulfilled? (To help you think more deeply about this, you might want to see our more detailed description of these needs in the Appendix on page 247.)**
- **When this need is threatened, how do you typically react? What default behavior can you recognize in yourself, and how does this behavior impact those around you? (For some examples of default behaviors, see below.)**

Imagine—or perhaps recall—how easy it is to associate common workplace situations with the needs noted above in a way that triggers a threat response. Countless situations can trigger a reactive response, but by way of illustration, here are some typical examples: The boss's bad mood can set off an entire department for days or weeks. Disgruntled stakeholders or negative comments by a colleague can likewise easily trigger us. Budget cuts are a classic trigger for those who see themselves as losers in a tug-of-war for limited resources, and a first cousin to this is the rumor mill that says massive layoffs are coming. Two additional triggers for many of us are the colleagues who don't deliver on commitments when you are counting on them, and being left out of the loop on issues or information you perceive as important to your success. We could all extend this list with our personal favorites, but hopefully, these examples indicate how subtle (and sometimes not so subtle) situations or experiences can grab us and push our threat buttons.

Understanding the kinds of situations that trigger us with an automatic response is helpful, but a resilient leader will also want to become more aware of what her/his reactive behaviors look like once s/he is triggered. The triad "fight, flight, freeze" has often been used to categorize the classic threat responses, but as noted above, our repertoire of automatic responses is not limited to those three. Perhaps you can identify the patterns of behavior you are most likely to fall into automatically when you are anxious by thinking about these examples:

- Make a decision hastily before gathering the facts
- Put off making a decision by seeking advice, even when you already have enough information
- Become more combative or confrontational
- Hide out in your office (or stay home) until the storm passes
- Micromanage everyone around you
- Underfunction in the hopes that someone else will take on the risk
- Put everything on hold until the threat passes
- Start blaming others for the threatening situation, without thinking about your part in the problem.

For a more thorough list of default behaviors, see the Reactive Behaviors Inventory on page 240 in the Appendix.

The kind of deep learning about anxiety (and the reactive behaviors that are its public face) is a great foundation. But that learning must be translated into a keener eye for how anxiety surfaces as reactivity in other individuals and in the various systems the leader is part of. As is true of the emotional system that lives within each of us, every organization, and every relationship network, has a measure of chronic anxiety that results in familiar patterns of reactive behavior. Astute leaders learn to recognize when anxiety is rising and becoming problematic by watching for typical patterns of reactivity in individuals and in the workplace at large, like the examples we've listed in the box below.

Here are some of the ways that reactivity often surfaces in organizations:

- Taking sides and forming cliques
- Turf battles, feuding and backstabbing
- Blaming and scapegoating
- Chronic overwork
- Higher accident rate or an increased use of sick leave
- Mixed messages from leadership
- People not saying what they really think
- Distancing – people hiding out in their offices
- Heavy turnover
- Taking things more seriously, less ability to use humor

This is tricky business because every person and every organization has a measure of anxiety and exhibits many of these patterns even in the best of times. It takes careful observation of reactive patterns over a period of time for a leader to be able to recognize when the emotional system is heating up and anxiety is reaching unhealthy levels that may require an intervention to cool things down. In prolonged or highly anxious times, a resilient leader may even be called upon simply to help the system manage its reactivity for as long as it takes until the system regains its equilibrium.

We worked with a leadership team in an organization that was deeply reengineering some of its fundamental structures of governance, product development, and marketing/sales. We did some preliminary training in the fundamentals of Resilient Leadership and then coached most of the senior leadership team over the two years when the changes were being planned and deployed. The CEO and the COO (who acted as the key drivers for the changes) came to be particularly astute observers of the reactive behaviors that ebbed and flowed as the changes were implemented. They learned to spot anxiety when it spiked in the two VPs responsible for the departments where the most radical restructuring was happening. And, more often than not, their steady, less anxious presence helped to keep those departments and their anxious leaders from slipping into reactive behaviors that could have done significant damage to the timeline.

Second Big Idea—A New Way of THINKING: Understand the contagious nature of a leader's presence.

In *The Proposal,* a popular comedy film from several years ago, Sandra Bullock plays an edgy, harsh manager of a public-relations firm who rules her organization with an iron fist. In one scene, she enters the main floor of her office and begins to walk through the hall on her way to fire someone. She doesn't say a word, but her demeanor is stiff, tense, and aloof, and as she passes by the cubicles, employees duck for cover and send covert messages to one another on their computers, like, "Watch out!" and, "The witch is on her broom!" While comical, the scene reminds us of how powerful a leader's presence is and how quickly it is read and spread by the people around him/her.

While a leader's actions are critical elements in achieving success, we believe that *a leader's primary lever for influencing emotional systems is the quality of his/her presence.* A positive presence, as we define it, is "the aura of confidence, poise, attentiveness, calm, focus, and energy that one radiates wherever one goes." It is the felt impact of a leader that permeates the organization and is keenly felt by everyone in the leader's system, even those who aren't nearby. As we saw in our opening story of Marissa, it is especially important for leaders to be present—both emotionally and physically—during anxious times.

A leader's primary lever for influencing emotional systems is the quality of his/her presense.

Bridgette worked with the CEO of a small but growing entrepreneurial company who complained to her one day about a puzzling spike in his leadership team's reactive behavior. He was disappointed at how its members had become testy with one another, were engaging in finger-pointing and scapegoating, and generally acting up. In recent years, his team had made progress in coming together and acting more collaboratively, so the recent turn both puzzled and frustrated him.

As they talked further, he shared with Bridgette that he had been gone for much of the summer with an unusual amount of travel and that when he was in the office, he had felt weighed down and distracted. It wasn't until Bridgette helped him to connect his absence from the office—and his lack of being emotionally present to the team when he was in the office—to the recent spike in reactivity, that he began to realize what was going on. His team members were acting up because they were anxious, and they were anxious because he had not been present, either physically or emotionally. What had been a puzzling and frustrating situation suddenly became clear and allowed him to see a new way to help his team calm down.

Emotional Contagion

Most of us have had similar experiences to the one in the movie, or in Bridgette's example above, where we have been "infected" by the negative energy of someone around us. Current research on emotional intelligence has revealed how powerfully contagious emotions are—much more so than we previously realized. *Emotional contagion* refers to the largely unconscious process by which we "catch" the moods and emotions of others. Neuroscience now helps to explain this phenomenon with the discovery of what are called mirror neurons. Thanks to mirror neurons, our brain picks up on the emotional state of another person (or group) in such a way that we actually experience in ourselves the same feeling state that we are being exposed to. Studies in which subjects were shown pictures of people they did not know, but whose faces expressed emotions such as fear or anger, revealed that the emotional centers of the brains of the research subjects lit up as if they themselves were afraid or angry.

Leaders' emotions are the most contagious of all because of where they sit in the organization.

Leaders' emotions are the most contagious of all because of where they sit in the organization and because of the close scrutiny that they are under by the people they lead. Bridgette's story above about the CEO whose team acted out while he was missing in action and was distracted with other concerns is a good example of the research finding that emotional contagion can significantly impair (or enhance) employee judgment, performance, and decision-making. Leaders who wish to function as step-down transformers for the systems they lead need to be aware of their moods and emotions and recognize how easily their negative energy can unwittingly make it more challenging for those around them to stay calm, positive, and thoughtful.

STOP & REFLECT

- **What words would you use to describe the *quality of your presence* in the last couple of weeks, as felt by your employees and other key stakeholders at work? Have you shown up as distracted? Energized? Anxious? Irritable? Enthused? Calm? Focused?**
- **What words would you use to describe the *quality of your presence* at home, as felt by your family and/or friends?**

Third Big Idea—A New Way of LEADING: Embody and communicate a less anxious presence.

In the pages above, we have given examples of the kind of leadership presence that we refer to as characteristic of a step-down transformer. In this Third Big Idea, we'd like to explore more deeply the nature of such a presence and how it is that a leader can learn to embody a less anxious presence as a core leadership competency. Such a person can embody and communicate an inner calm in a way that helps others to lower their own anxiety. It may sound simple (though, of course, it's not), but all that it takes for a leader to act as a step-down transformer is to be less anxious than those around her/him. But, how to do that when everyone around us is acting as a step-up transformer?

Calming the Body

Let's start with some basics: When we are anxious, our body immediately signals distress in many subtle—and sometimes not-so-subtle—ways. The polygraph that measures key biometrics operates on the principle that most people are not consciously aware of—let alone able to mask—those subtle bodily changes when they are anxious about being caught in a lie. Similarly, specialists in reading body language have cataloged a list of key indicators that are below conscious awareness but to the trained eye can signal a range of emotions and moods. The good news is that if we pay attention, we can learn to spot many of the bodily signs of heightened anxiety in ourselves. And, once we realize that our body is carrying that anxiety, we can work on calming ourselves by deliberately relaxing our body.

What, then, are some of the frequent bodily indicators of anxiety? For some people, raised shoulders and a slight curving in of the body (to protect vital organs), or an effort to shrink in size (as if to avoid being a target) can be telltale signs of anxiety. For many, shallow breathing and tension in the jaw, back, chest, neck, or stomach are common signals of inner tension. These are all common ways we embody anxiety, and if we pay attention to what our body is telling us, we can lower anxiety by taking countermeasures that can help to calm our anxious mind and feelings.

Many simple physical moves can relax our body and help us manage and roll back our anxiety. One practice that we suggest because it can be done virtually anytime or anyplace is what we call six-second centering. We describe this simple Core Practice at the end of this chapter, and we invite you to consider making it a routine part of your day. We have taught six-second centering to hundreds of leaders, and the vast majority of them find it to be an invaluable way to calm their nervous system so that they can think more clearly and creatively about the challenges and/or threats that are causing them to feel anxious in the first place.

Many other physical-relaxation practices are also worth exploring and can be done before, during, or after times of heightened anxiety. But even more helpful may be preventative steps that help us remain calm so that our level of chronic anxiety never reaches too high a level.

Here is a sampling of the many preventive practices that leaders we have worked with have used to maintain a less anxious presence:

- Develop a repertoire of activities that help you to center yourself (e.g., exercise, yoga, meditation/mindfulness, etc.)
- Take care of the basics that are foundational to emotional bandwidth, like getting enough exercise and sleep, and eating properly
- Focus on/get in touch with your strengths and who you are at your best
- Reconnect with the noble purpose of your life to gain perspective
- Keep a reflective journal
- Find support systems that help you to relax and become more thoughtful (e.g., coaching, therapy, peer groups, mentors)
- Talk with a trusted colleague about what is raising your level of anxiety

As we said earlier in this section, a leader who is a less anxious presence is someone who embodies and communicates an inner calm in a way that helps others to lower their anxiety. Doing so paves the way for clear thinking to prevail. So far, we've focused our attention primarily on the first half of this equation—to embody an inner calm—but the latter half, how we *communicate* with anxious others, is what we turn our attention to now.

Communicating a Calm Presence

Sometimes a simple change in how we communicate is all it takes to begin the process of calming an anxious system. Bob's experience with a senior team of a high-tech company that was in the midst of rolling out massive changes to key processes *and* a sweeping reorganization is a good example of this. Not surprisingly, the organization was experiencing a rise in both acute and chronic anxiety, and many employees (including some of the members of the senior team) were displaying the kind of reactive behaviors we discussed in this chapter. Knowing that it was up to them as leaders to calm the system, they asked Bob to share with them some strategies for how they could communicate more effectively as step-down transformers and bring some measure of calm to a highly reactive system. Bob shared with the team the behaviors and communication strategies you see below and asked every leader to pick one to commit to practicing over the next month as the process and reorganization changes were rolled out.

How to communicate as a Step-Down Transformer:

- Be quick to observe, listen, and be curious, rather than react
- Use playfulness to lessen tension in self and others and don't take yourself too seriously
- Ask questions to gain better perspective, deeper awareness and to build common understanding. Try to reframe the issue
- Invite the group to step back and see the bigger picture of how they may be contributing to things, by posing the question, "What's our role in this?"
- Focus others on the facts, rather than assumptions, judgments, and gossip
- Bring clarity to the rational system by communicating and regularly clarifying roles, goals, and priorities (for more on this, see Chapter 3 on Lead with Conviction)

When he met with the team a month later, one senior leader spoke about how he had decided to become a "curious questioner" rather than a "know-it-all leader." Instead of succumbing to the pressure he felt to supply the answer to every problem or question his employees brought to him, he practiced asking questions from a place of genuine curiosity to draw out the facts and their own best thinking. In doing so, he reported a significant drop in their level of anxiety and reactivity, and also in his own.

Asking questions from a place of curiosity is a powerful way to lower anxiety and bring greater thoughtfulness to a situation. In fact, neuroscience research tells us that it is next to impossible to be both curious and anxious at the same time! That said, asking questions alone is not enough. We've all been at the receiving end of interrogation, which is all about asking questions, but not from an open, curious stance. *Inquiry*, on the other hand, means "to inquire from a place of openness" and requires a willingness on our part to be influenced by what we hear. Leaders who act as step-down transformers understand this distinction and work to practice skillful inquiry rather than interrogation. The example above underscores how adopting even one of these step-down transformer practices can make a big difference. From a systems perspective, this makes sense, as what affects one affects all.

The Difference between Urgency and Anxiety

While chronic anxiety (and the reactivity it provokes) often makes things worse by interfering with our capacity for calm, clear, thoughtful action, urgency, on the other hand, can contribute to making a difficult problem or situation better. Anxiety makes clear thinking less likely, has a frenetic quality to it, and spreads like wildfire. Urgency is focused, purposeful, and steady—a relentless yet thoughtful pursuit of important goals and priorities and a call to action in the face of critical threats or vital opportunities. A leader who cultivates a sense of urgency focuses people on what matters most, clearly articulates the need for change, and galvanizes people to act. An effective leader learns how to operate as a calming influence during anxious times, lowering anxiety and reactivity in the system, yet also promoting a sense of urgency when and where it is needed. To better understand the difference between increasing urgency versus raising anxiety, see page 253 in the Appendix.

STOP & REFLECT

- **Take a look at the tips on how to communicate as a step-down transformer above and notice which ones you already do regularly. Which one might you pick to add to your routine of practices so that you can strengthen your ability to bring a calming influence to those around you?**

Core Practices

Six-Second Centering

Use six-second centering before and during important meetings and conversations to cultivate a calmer, clearer, and more credible presence. This short practice gives us a simple way to calm our physiology, which is the first step toward bringing a less anxious, more thoughtful mindset to our day. Here's how it works:

- **Two seconds.** Uncross your legs and feel your feet firmly on the floor. The act of feeling your feet into the floor grounds you in the present moment and unhooks you from the emotional or mental storytelling that gives rise to reactivity.
- **Two seconds.** Inhale deeply; lengthen your spine and embody an upright posture as you breathe in fully. When we sit or stand with an upright posture (versus slumping), we telegraph confidence, credibility, and calm.
- **Two seconds.** Exhale slowly, relaxing your jaw, shoulders, and chest. Feel your feet into the floor, to once again ground yourself in the present moment. Anxiety is often stored in the body in our shoulders, jaw, and chest. Relaxing these areas as you exhale releases stored stress, helps to lower cortisol levels (the stress hormone) and enables you to project greater poise.

Cultivate a Curious Mind-Set

It is almost impossible to be both curious and anxious at the same time!

- When you observe anxiety and reactivity surfacing during meetings (either in yourself or in others), step back and be curious.
- Without judgment, ask questions from a place of genuine curiosity about what is happening, and be open to what you see and hear.

Chapter Summary

- A leader who acts as a step-down transformer brings a calming influence to an anxious family, team, or organization. Every leader, at every level, can learn to be more of a step-down transformer by intentionally working on self-management.
- The first step toward becoming a step-down transformer is to become a more astute observer of reactivity—the public face of anxiety. By observing with curiosity how we, and those around us, automatically react to perceived threats, we can create new possibilities for more thoughtful action.
- The quality of a leader's presence is highly contagious and is the primary lever for influence. A positive presence is the aura of confidence, poise, attentiveness, calm, focus, and energy that one radiates wherever one goes.
- Too much anxiety—either within us or around us—interferes with clear thinking and innovation. The good news is that a leader does not need to be free of all anxiety to have a calming effect on an anxious system. All that is required is for the leader to be less anxious than others in the system.
- A leader who exudes a less anxious presence embodies and communicates an inner calm in a way that helps others lower their anxiety.
- Neuroscience reveals that it is almost impossible to be both curious and anxious at the same time. A thoughtful leader can capitalize on this finding by being quick to observe, to listen, and to be curious, rather than immediately react. Doing so paves the way for clear thinking to prevail.
- A Resilient Leader understands the difference between raising a sense of urgency versus escalating anxious reactivity. The former is focused, purposeful, and steady while the latter is frenetic, catches like wildfire, and makes clear thinking less likely.

CHAPTER 3

LEAD WITH CONVICTION
ACT BOLDLY IN THE FACE OF INCREASING COMPLEXITY AND ESCALATING CHANGE

> Leadership through self-differentiation is not easy; learning techniques and imbibing data are far easier. Nor is striving or achieving success as a leader without pain: there is the pain of isolation, the pain of loneliness, the pain of personal attacks, the pain of losing friends. That's what leadership is all about.
>
> —Edwin Friedman
> *A Failure of Nerve*

Bill had recently been promoted from within to the top slot in a large nonprofit service provider that had seen a significant drop in revenues over the past two-plus years. This was the first time he had been "alone at the top," as he put it, and he now had to deal with an overbearing and demanding board chair who was well-known for micromanaging every time he was worried about some real or imagined threat. This time the threat was real, and he demanded of Bill a quick solution to the declining revenues, adding ominously, "Or else we're going to be looking at some pretty big layoffs." To make matters worse, the board chair had made the threat of layoffs in a public forum, and the anxiety of the workforce was escalating daily.

Bill's "solution" was to convoke the entire board and senior team in a two-day, off-site strategic-planning retreat focused on meeting the fiscal challenge. He had hired a top-notch (and quite expensive) facilitator for the retreat whose specialty was helping organizations such as Bill's to recover from declining revenues. Just before the retreat began, the board chair pulled Bill aside and said, "I saw how much you're paying this gal. She better be worth it."

What's Going On Here?

Bill was anxious not only about the success of the upcoming strategic planning session but also about his ability to perform well as the top leader in his organization. In addition, he was dealing with a highly anxious (and therefore not very thoughtful) system, including virtually all of the board and the vice presidents who reported to him.

Despite the anxiety swirling around (and in) him, Bill managed to do something that required a great deal of courage and stamina—he took a risk that made him vulnerable to ridicule and failure. The chair of the board had made it clear right before the planning session began how much was at stake for Bill with his decision, including his reputation with the board and perhaps even their ongoing support of him.

Bill knew that a bold move was needed to turn his organization around and that if it was going to create a new future, it would be up to him to lead it there. He had wrestled with the central dilemma facing the company (i.e., declining membership) and had done a great deal of reading and reflection in order to determine the right way forward. While he was convinced that a big part of the solution was to refocus the board and his senior team on a new way of envisioning the future, he was keenly aware that his decision to hire an outside facilitator (and to change the way they had always done strategic planning) could blow up in his face. If it did, he would have nowhere to hide.

> To **Lead with Conviction** means to act boldly, take clear stands, and be willing to take risks (even when it makes you vulnerable to failure and ridicule) for the sake of preserving core values and/or creating a future you care about.

Bill's willingness to act boldly, even though it made him vulnerable to failure and ridicule, is the essence of what it means to lead with conviction. Doing so is never easy, and it can be especially challenging when the system's level of chronic anxiety is on the rise.

Let's take a look at how anxiety can derail even the best of leaders from taking the bold action that is needed to lead their organizations to new levels of effectiveness and success.

First Big Idea—A New Way of SEEING: Recognize when anxiety—in yourself or in your system—makes it more challenging to lead with conviction.

The context of this Big Idea is the New Way of SEEING, and in particular, it is about the ability of a leader to recognize anxiety—especially chronic anxiety that is high and growing even higher—in self and in the system. Recall that we refer to reactivity as the public face of anxiety—a face that reveals to us what is happening at the deeper levels of the emotional system where chronic anxiety churns beneath the surface of conscious awareness in the form of automatic, instinctive functioning and habitual patterns. Observing anxiety, then, is about observing reactivity. The core insight of this Big Idea highlights the fact that leading with conviction when anxiety is high in self, the organization—or both—can be extremely challenging.

It is the nature of an anxious system to become risk averse, despite the fact that bold steps are often required when substantial threats loom on the horizon. A resilient leader who is convinced that courageous action is needed must be able to resist the pressure to play it safe or to wait it out. Often, the trusted advisors who are closest to the leader in such times become the leader's greatest obstacle to taking the kinds of steps most needed to rescue the organization from a downward spiral. The story of Bill at the beginning of this chapter describes how difficult a challenge it can be for a leader to take a bold step when an anxious organization is shouting in a single chorus, *"Play it safe!"*

Dealing with a risk-averse culture under such circumstances is perplexing and exhausting. A leader who knows the importance of staying connected to the organization in anxious times will need to work overtime to resist being infected by the fears and reactive behaviors of those around her or him. Higher than usual resolve and stamina are required to keep from exhausting one's interior resources and falling into the surrounding herd mentality. Precisely at the point where clarity of thinking and a calm, thoughtful focus are most needed to manage an overheated system, a leader will find it extraordinarily challenging to do so.

In the story above, if Bill had allowed himself to become overfocused on the anxieties of the board chair, his ability to take the decisive action described would surely have been severely compromised. Instead, he managed his own anxiety and proved himself capable of out-of-the-box thinking that offered reasonable hope of turning a failing organization around at a critical juncture. But we can imagine the inner turmoil Bill was feeling. He was a new leader; he was not very confident that he had what it took to lead a failing organization out of danger. And his bold move was not a sure thing—it well might have failed and brought a premature end to Bill's leadership role.

Other stakeholders besides the board also might have cautioned Bill against the move he was contemplating. His leadership team might have reminded him that there was already a tried-and-true process for doing strategic planning, and it was inclusive of many voices that would not be present for Bill's new idea of a two-day retreat. What if some key partners rebelled because they had been left out of the loop? Or what if he had overlooked some crucial information or a set of stakeholders that would be essential for the success of any solution? The voices within Bill's head and all around him were conceivably so challenging that he could easily have succumbed to the pressure. But he did not!

STOP & REFLECT

- **Think of a time when you acted boldly or took a risk despite the fears and anxiety swirling around you or in you.**
- **What resources did you draw upon to resist being "infected" by the fears or anxieties of others? How did you gather your resolve?**

Second Big Idea—A New Way of THINKING: Understand the crucial role a leader's clarity of vision, values, and principles plays in calming an anxious system.

One of the universal truths of "thinking systems" is that a lack of clarity in the rational system provokes reactivity in the emotional system. People crave clarity, especially in anxious times, and especially from their leader. If a system's anxiety has been raised due to a bold move on the part of the leader, it is all the more important to connect that move to the leader's vision, core values, and guiding principles. When a leader is good at communicating that connection to the members of the organization, the system tends to calm down, become more thoughtful, and better able to focus on and pursue its mission.

We have already indicated that our description of a resilient leader is rooted in Murray Bowen's notion of self-differentiation, and it may be helpful to review here what self-differentiation means and why it is essential to effective leadership. *Self-differentiation* refers to an individual's capacity for independent thought and action (self-definition) while maintaining a balanced connection to significant others (self-regulation). Our shorthand way of capturing this definition is "lead with conviction and stay connected."

In Chapter 4, we expand on the notion of what it means to stay connected; here, our focus is on how being a clear, well-defined leader equips one to lead with greater conviction and boldness, particularly in challenging, anxious situations.

Clarity of vision and values, remaining committed to personal and organizational goals, and consistently acting on one's principles are essential ingredients. So, too, is the ability to stand apart from the emotional climate of the system to which the leader belongs. This is a lifelong task that involves stepping back regularly (what we and others refer to as "getting on the balcony") to become more observant, more thoughtful, and calmer. Working on one's self-differentiation is a process of striving to become more of a "self" by thoughtfully defining who we are, what we value, and where we stand—and then communicating that to others in a way that makes it easier for them to follow our lead.

STOP & REFLECT

- **To what extent are your vision, core values, and guiding principles clear to you and to those you lead?**
- **How might you lead with greater clarity and consistency?**

Being a clear, well-defined, and consistent leader is not always easy in today's high-pressure workplace, where leaders can be thrown off course by the many competing, and often conflicting, demands they must face.

Tom's Story

Several years ago, Bridgette coached Tom, the leader of a highly successful family-owned business that was in talks with another organization interested in either a merger or a buyout. The talks were supposed to be strictly confidential, but due to leaks from the other organization, it had become common knowledge, and anxiety in Tom's company was spreading top to bottom over fears that job elimination and / or significant layoffs might result.

Tom was highly principled and deeply committed to his very loyal employees. He had no intention of cutting a deal that would result in layoffs, but he had agreed not to disclose to anyone even the fact that talks were underway. He also was aware of how harmful it was to allow his employees' unfounded fears to continue to spread and raise anxiety even further. Tom also understood his responsibility to support the emotional health of the system, and in what was a very bold move during the delicate talks, he halted the process and renegotiated his confidentiality agreement to allow him to (1) acknowledge to his employees that talks were underway that could potentially bring great benefit to their company and (2) reassure his employees that the talks were about growth possibilities and that layoffs were not part of any eventual deal.

Calmly and with great conviction, he communicated those two points to his employees in a way that could have made him the poster child for our Second Big Idea. Because of the deep trust Tom had earned from his employees over many years, they believed him and took him at his word that their jobs were not imminently at risk. The result was a dramatic drop in anxiety, a shift in the mood of the organization, and a surge in productivity as his team ramped up its performance to show what a great company they had.

Being a clear, well-defined, and consistent leader is important regardless of your level in the organization. Whether you are a CEO or a first-time supervisor, communicating your vision, values, and guiding principles helps others to know what to expect from you and what you expect from them.

Third Big Idea—A New Way of LEADING: In the face of resistance and sabotage, stay the course—without feeling defensive or needing to win.

Annette, a former client of Bob, called upon him to help her remain thoughtful during a very challenging change-management initiative she had been hired to lead. The board of a high-tech organization had hired her as CEO with a strong mandate to "change the company culture" from a highly siloed organization with too much internal competition and too little collaboration or communication across divisions. Annette's hire coincided with a long-planned relocation of the corporate offices, and she had decided to use the move as an opportunity to send a strong signal that silos were no longer going to be allowed to stand.

Her plan—well underway when Bob first met with her—involved designing an innovative office space where no one—not even the senior leadership team—had their own private office space. "No more closed doors" was the mantra Annette had used to convey to her leadership team that they were being charged with engaging in a degree of collaboration and cross-division communication that would jump-start a more innovative, nimble reset of the organizational culture.

In their first coaching session, Annette unloaded on Bob her anger at two members of her team in particular. Both had been quietly voicing to everyone but Annette their dislike of the new office plan, always concluding with a pessimistic, "There's no way this crazy idea will work!" In anxious tones, she shared with Bob her sense of betrayal at their disloyalty and that she was going to call them out at the next meeting of the senior team, which she had scheduled for the following morning in her office despite the fact that the next regularly scheduled meeting was two weeks away. As she remarked to Bob, "I will not have sabotage!"

What's Going On Here?

Annette's story is emblematic of many of the situations leaders share with us as they attempt to lead change. Inevitably, they bump up against resistance that feels like deliberate sabotage, and they often struggle with how to respond. What might we learn from Annette's situation if we look at her reactions (and those of her team) through the lens of Resilient Leadership? Here are a few observations worth considering:

- A self-differentiating move is an action or position you take that charts a new course for you, your team, and/or your organization and is based on a thoughtful consideration of your vision, values, and guiding principles.
- Annette's decision to radically redesign the office space is what we call a "self-differentiating move," as are what Bill in the First Big Idea and Tom in the Second Big Idea did. Such moves are essential to leading with conviction, and they require not only a great deal of clarity on the part of a leader but skillful execution as well.
- A leader's self-differentiating move almost always provokes resistance (sabotage), most often from the less well-differentiated parts of the system. This is so because systems are designed by their very nature to maintain the status quo—even when change is badly needed.

- Such sabotage often feels intensely personal, as it did to Annette (after all, the poison arrows seemed to be aimed directly at her), and she got hooked into reacting without pausing to notice her own anxiety or to manage her own anxious response.
- Annette's emotional reactivity led her to hyper-focus on squelching the dissenters instead of calmly and firmly redefining her stance.

STOP & REFLECT

- **Think of a time when you made a self-differentiating move as a leader. What can you recall about the courage it took for you to do so?**
- **How did others respond to your self-differentiating move? If you faced resistance or sabotage, were you able to stay the course?**

Reactive versus Productive Complaints

One of the hardest things to do when facing resistance / sabotage is to distinguish between reactive and productive complaints. A reactive complaint is one that is made at the wrong time to the wrong person and with the wrong tone. A productive complaint, on the other hand, is made at the right time to the right person and with the right tone. The latter should be listened to, while the former is rarely ever about the content of the complaint itself. Rather, a reactive complaint is best understood as a signal that chronic anxiety is on the rise within a system.

Productive Complaints:

- Arise out of a genuine interest to help
- Involve thoughtful possible solutions
- Are expressed from a calm, centered place
- Bring a curious and objective view of all aspects of the problem
- Are focused on creating a shared path forward

Reactive Complaints:

- Arise out of fear-based anxiety
- Have content that is not what it's really about
- Are expressed from an un-centered, anxious place

Were the grumblings by two members of Annette's senior team thoughtful concerns that she should listen to, or reactive complaints? Upon further reflection, Annette wasn't sure, and with Bob's help she decided to take a step back and reconsider her next moves. She was reminded that only by remaining (relatively) calm and nonreactive can a leader hope to distinguish between reactive sabotage and thoughtful opposition.

The Rest of Annette's Story

Annette did remain firm in her intent to design a more collaborative workspace. She was convinced it was an essential part of the needed culture change, and she continued to articulate with resolve her vision and the role she expected her team to play as leaders in the effort.

She never called out her two passive-aggressive team members. Instead, she asked the two of them to work together to collect employee concerns about the new plan and present her with possible solutions, along with their recommendations. She made it clear to them what was open for consideration and what was not so that the boundaries of their potential recommendations were clearly drawn.

In the end, she was able to accept enough of their recommendations about how to smooth the way to change that they soon found themselves invested in the success of the project. One final takeaway that Annette learned is that a system's need for strong leadership is quite often sufficient to overcome the natural inclination to resist change.

A Final Note

Edwin Friedman, from whom Bob learned about the work of Murray Bowen, often spoke about how important it was for a self-differentiating leader to persist in the face of sabotage. If such a leader could make the right moves when confronted with resistance, it was what Ed called "the key to the kingdom." Friedman not only spoke about the inevitability of sabotage; he believed it was a sign that the leader was actually doing something right! We concur with his assessment and encourage leaders we work with to see their self-differentiating moves, and the resulting sabotage they provoke, as positive indications of their leadership. Rather than being something to fear, suppress, or avoid, a resilient leader can expect and even learn to embrace sabotage as part and parcel of the process of leadership itself.

Core Practices

Communicate Where You Stand
Remember that communication is almost entirely an emotional phenomenon—only a small fraction of the experience is about conveying objective information. Whenever there is confusion around an important issue, step back and thoughtfully consider where you stand on it—both how you think and how you feel about it—irrespective of the emotional pressures you might be feeling. Then communicate your stand calmly, clearly, and nondefensively.

Embody Your Length
Whenever you have to take a tough stand on a difficult issue, embody your length (assume a tall, upright posture) and continue to do so especially if and when you get pushback. Embodying your length (assuming a tall spine) exemplifies dignity, communicates confidence and credibility, and supports holding your ground under pressure.

Recent research by Amy Cuddy shows that expansive postures can increase the level of testosterone in our bodies (which is the hormone associated with increased confidence) and lower the level of cortisol (which is the stress hormone).

Chapter Summary

- *Leading with conviction* means to "act boldly, even when doing so makes you vulnerable to ridicule and failure." This requires the courage to stand apart and even to stand alone. Leadership is often a lonely pursuit, and the best leaders learn to embrace its solitude.
- A leader's self-differentiating move always provokes resistance (sabotage) from the system. Resilient leaders learn to expect resistance and sabotage as part and parcel of leadership itself, even coming to recognize it as a sign that they are doing something right!
- Staying the course, without getting defensive or needing to win, requires stamina. For this reason, resilient leaders know how to take good care of themselves—mentally, physically, emotionally, and spiritually.
- A lack of clarity in the rational system provokes reactivity in the emotional system. For this reason, clarity and consistency are two of the most important attributes leaders can cultivate. Both act as calming agents on an anxious system.
- Acting in a way that is aligned with one's goals, mission, vision, and guiding principles is vital to leading with conviction. Doing so requires that leaders intentionally create reflective time in their day/week and vigorously guard that time from competing demands and distractions.
- Not all complaints are equal! Reactive complaints are a sign of anxiety and usually aren't even about the content of the complaint itself. Resilient leaders avoid being hooked by reactive complaints and instead teach their employees to make productive complaints, which are thoughtful, keep the big picture in mind, and are voiced from a centered place.

CHAPTER 4

STAY CONNECTED
FORGE HEALTHY, BALANCED RELATIONSHIPS WITH THOSE YOU LEAD

Relationship work, paradoxically, is a solitary project. It may feel like growing a self. It is not necessary, important, or even possible to work on the other person.

—Roberta Gilbert
Extraordinary Relationships

John was a new manager who had recently been promoted out of his peer group to manage the business analyst group in his company. He was an excellent analyst, had "good people skills" according to his manager, and was given the role of lead supervisor when his own manager left for another position. However, John had been given very little training in how to supervise or manage others and was somewhat anxious about his ability to succeed in this new role. One of the people he supervised had applied for the role that John now had and clearly wasn't happy about the outcome. Several of the other employees now under John's supervision had been close friends of his, and they had enjoyed a great deal of camaraderie as teammates on the company softball team.

Although he did not reveal this to anyone, John felt conflicted in his new role. He wasn't sure how to supervise his former friends, and, truth be told, he missed being "one of the gang." On the other hand, he was ambitious, and this new role afforded him not only an increase in salary but also an opportunity to further his career. At the end of his first week as manager, one of John's employees invited him to happy hour with the rest of the team. He agreed to go but felt uneasy about it. He knew that they were likely to drink too much and gossip about various changes in the office that were underway. On the other hand, he didn't want to seem aloof or "too big for his own britches," as his mother was fond of saying.

John was caught between two impulses, each of which tugged at him with equal strength—the desire to be liked and to remain on friendly terms with those he now supervised, and the desire to assert himself in his new role. In the first few months that John was in his new supervisor role, his boss noticed that he seemed a bit conflicted and hesitant to lead his peers, and he wondered if John was cut out for the job after all.

What's Going On Here?

Those who transition from peer-group contributor to supervisor often feel John's sense of unease. This transition in the life of a leader can feel like an identity crisis as a new leader struggles to let go of the status and satisfaction s/he once enjoyed as an expert while not yet fully understanding how to succeed in a new role. But the unease that John felt was a result of even deeper forces that he was only partly aware of at the time.

Within the context of all relationships, individuals are driven to meet two fundamental needs: the need to be close (togetherness) and the need to be separate (individuality). How well we strike the right balance between these two needs ultimately determines the health and vitality of our relationships, both at work and on the home front. John's inner conflict was a result of the tension he felt between these two needs, which he now had to learn to balance in a different way if he was going to be effective in leading others.

Finding the Middle Ground

Because of the position that a leader occupies within the relationship system of an organization, how well that leader strikes a balance between the two fundamental forces of togetherness and individuality plays a decisive role in the functioning of the entire organization. The ancient adage that "virtue is to be found in the middle" holds true here as well. Good organizational health—just like good individual health—is the result of finding the middle course between being close without becoming enmeshed, all the while staying separate without becoming isolated.

That said, finding this middle ground can be elusive for leaders, as it was for John. Staying connected in a balanced and healthy way requires a keen awareness about how we tend to function under stress, along with a deliberate and thoughtful effort to strike just the right balance with our various stakeholders.

In Chapter 1 we said that there are three imperatives that capture the essence of what it looks like to show up with a well-differentiated leadership presence: **Stay Calm, Stay the Course,**

Stay Connected. The first two are essential, but if a leader does not know how to stay connected, mastery of the first two will be for naught. The 3 Big Ideas that follow will introduce you to the insights that helped John (and many of the other leaders we have worked with) to stay connected in just the right way.

First Big Idea—A New Way of SEEING: Observe whether your default tendency is toward too much distance or too much closeness.

Bridgette often tells a delightful story about her son at age five, sitting at his bench, intently working in his coloring book. It was nearing dinnertime, and Bridgette had asked him several times to put away his things and wash his hands, yet he remained fixed on his coloring. Finally, she raised her voice to get his attention, telling him it was time now to stop. He stood up, looked at her fiercely, and with great intensity said to her, "I need to be my own person!"

Every parent knows that well before the age of five, the primal need to be an independent self is already a force to be reckoned with in their young child. So, too, is the child's compelling need to be connected, to be held close, and to receive the assurance that comes from the parent's gestures and words of approval. These drives for autonomy and intimacy are not early-childhood stages that we outgrow. They remain with us throughout our lives, reinventing themselves in countless forms of expression at each and every life-cycle stage and in all the various situations in which we find ourselves.

> **The drives for autonomy and intimacy are not early childhood stages that we outgrow. They remain with us throughout our lives, reinventing themselves in countless forms.**

Careful study of these drives has established several insights that are relevant to this Big Idea. Along the continuum between being close and being distant, each of us has a default preference whose origins lie both in individual personality factors and in the family system we were part of as we grew up. We carry that default tendency into the workplace, and it significantly shapes how we operate as leaders. Beneath our conscious awareness, both in our personal and in our professional lives, each of us is constantly assessing our current reality and trying to strike the right balance between our need to be separate and our need to be close. But whichever may be our default tendency, specific details of different situations can always incline us toward the opposite direction. Both directions remain part of our repertoire, and either one can be to the fore in any given circumstance.

Avoid the Extremes

Research has also shown that when we are highly anxious, we tend to move toward the extreme form of one tendency or the other: toward too much distance if we tend to prefer autonomy; toward too much closeness if we tend toward intimacy. The higher the anxiety, the stronger the pull toward the extremes.

On the close-distant continuum, a *cutoff* is the extreme version of distancing. When we cut off from a relationship system (whether that is with one individual or an entire group), we withdraw from those involved (either physically or emotionally). The impact of a leader cutting off from one or more of an organization's stakeholders is significant, because, as we will see with the next Big Idea, a leader can only positively influence a system to which s/he is connected. *Thus, a cutoff results in a loss of influence.* Few leaders recognize this, because distancing ourselves from a contentious, anxious, or demanding stakeholder often feels better in the short term, while it is easy to ignore that the cutoff will make our job more challenging in the long run.

When leaders fuse with others, they become entangled emotionally and less differentiated from those they are leading.

The extreme of too much closeness is known as "fusion." When leaders fuse with others, they become entangled emotionally and are less *differentiated from* those they are leading. As a result, they can easily lose their capacity to stand apart from the crowd, to make tough decisions that might negatively impact others, and, ultimately, to be recognized as the leader in charge. Thus, like cutoff, *fusion also results in a loss of influence,* but for different reasons.

Recognize Your Default Tendency

While cutoff and fusion represent the extremes, the New Way of SEEING we are speaking about here is being able to recognize whether your default tendency as a leader is toward too much closeness or too much distance. Perhaps you already have a sense of which direction you tend to go when you feel stress in your relationship systems. But to help you more clearly recognize your default tendency, here are some behaviors associated with the tendency toward *too much closeness*: A first indicator is that you tend to take sides with another person or group consistently without figuring out where you as an individual stand. Another red flag is identifying with another's pain or problem excessively, to the point that it starts to impact your own functioning. The root cause here is that you have become so emotionally enmeshed with the other(s) that you lose perspective and can no longer tell where you end and they begin. Finally, these tendencies often result in your feeling so responsible for what belongs to the other(s) that you start to overfunction and they start to underfunction.

By way of contrast, here are some behaviors associated with the tendency toward *too much distance:* A first indicator is that you feel a pull to withdraw from anxious relationships, either emotionally or physically. One way this can surface in a workplace is that you find yourself checking out in a meeting, especially when someone with whom you have a conflict is speaking. Spending excessive amounts of time in your own office (or out of the office altogether) is another expression of this tendency, as is the temptation to leave people with whom you are at odds out of the loop on important e-mails or not include them in relevant meetings. Finally, a consistent pattern of looking for points of disagreement—or bad-mouthing or complaining about another person or group with whom you disagree—is a form of reactive distancing.

STOP & REFLECT

- **Based on what you have read so far, what do you think is your default tendency at work when you are anxious: toward too much closeness (fusion) or too much distance (cutoff)?**
- **What is the impact of your default tendency on those you lead?**
- **What is your default tendency at home when you are anxious: toward too much closeness or too much distance? What is the impact on those you live with?**

We mentioned earlier in this chapter that good organizational health (like good individual health) is related to how well its members achieve a proper balance between individuality and togetherness. Too much separateness can lead to various parts of an organization or teams operating as isolated silos. Too much togetherness can lead to groupthink and a diminished capacity for risk-taking and creative problem-solving.

How Your Default Influences the Organization

Relationship systems tend to follow their leader in this regard, as in so many other aspects of organizational life. Thus, the New Way of SEEING is not only about being able to spot your own default tendency, but noticing how your way of operating is influencing your organization/team as a whole.

Imagine for a moment a leader whose default tendency when anxious leans toward too much distance. What kinds of workplace behaviors might we see proliferating in this leader's system when anxiety levels rise? Here are a few predictable expressions of organizational distancing that we might see:

- Closed doors; people hiding out or not available
- Withdrawal of certain teams or groups from regular communication with other groups/teams
- Withholding of certain information from people to control the situation
- Increased levels of people checking out or disengaging
- Targeting certain individuals for cutoffs and justifying it by blaming them for the problems or challenges being faced
- A heavier, more serious mood that pervades the system

And what if a leader's default tendency when anxious leans toward too much closeness? Here are some of the workplace behaviors we might see proliferating in that leader's system when stress and anxiety are on the rise:

- Water-cooler gossip and blaming
- Increased emotional intensity in longer-than-usual e-mail chains with lots of cc's and bcc's
- More than the usual amount of drama over perceived slights or miscommunication

- Meeting after meeting with very little progress made on real issues
- People anxiously inserting themselves into areas that aren't theirs to manage
- Groupthink and herding with no one individual willing to go against the prevailing tide

Any movement in an organization in the direction of the extremes of cutoff or fusion is symptomatic of elevated levels of anxiety. Ironically, both extremes of behavior share a common foundation: they are attempts to preserve the integrity of self (i.e., the core identity of the organization) when feeling threatened by too much closeness or too much distance. These workplace behaviors are simply the adult version of the cry of Bridgette's young son: *"I need to be my own person!"*

The point here is to pay attention to when and how others in your organization tend toward one or the other extreme when anxious and be quick to intervene by drawing them out of themselves and engaging with them (if they tend to isolate) or by encouraging them to take a step back and take some time apart before fueling others' anxieties (if they tend to become enmeshed in the reactivity of the group).

STOP & REFLECT

- **Think about each of your direct reports and what their default tendency might be. As you consider this, are any of them drawing too close or being too distant from those they are managing?**

- **If so, how might you help them adjust their functioning so that they can find the middle ground between being connected yet not enmeshed while being separate yet not isolated?**

Second Big Idea—A New Way of THINKING: Understand that a leader is only able to exert positive influence on a system to which s/he is connected.

Bob was called by a former client, Teresa, to help her address some growing problems with the members of her leadership team. Teresa ran a small company and had always had excellent working relationships with her entire workforce, especially with her senior team. As she explained to Bob in their first meeting, the team had been challenging her on several initiatives she was trying to get started, complaining they were already working at capacity and just didn't have the bandwidth for anything new. Bob knew from his previous work with Teresa and the team that they were all highly creative and loved the challenge of undertaking new projects. Teresa insisted to Bob that they were not any busier at present than they had ever been, yet now it seemed like lately, they were pushing back on her ideas at every turn.

Bob asked Teresa to describe to him what had been happening that might have impacted the emotional system in the last six months—any outside pressures, any changes of personnel, any looming threats, and so forth. Teresa found it hard to come up with anything of significance, and at one point when Bob pressed her on the details of a particular situation, she responded, "Honestly, Bob, I'm not sure about any of that. I've been distracted a good bit of the time over the past few months, and I just haven't been able to keep on top of all of the details like I used to."

Bob was curious and asked, "Really? Why is that?" Teresa hesitated and then got up and walked over to shut her office door. In hushed tones, she said, "Bob, this is strictly between us. My husband came down with cancer about three or four months ago, and it's been a real roller coaster. He made me promise not to tell anyone about his battle, but I've been picking up the pieces at home for months—taking him to one doctor after another, seeing him through chemo and radiation, and running the kids to all of their activities. It's been exhausting. But as far as everyone here is concerned, nothing has changed other than that I may seem more exhausted than ever before."

For Bob, hearing this revelation was like having a light go on in a dark room. He offered words of support and compassion for what Teresa and her family were going through, and then he began to explain to Teresa the connection between her diverted attention away from the office, the compromised quality of her presence when she was there, and the resistance she was meeting from her senior team. Initially, Teresa pushed back, insisting that she was keeping up with all of her core responsibilities, even when it meant working far into the night. Bob then explained to her that the anxiety she was feeling for her husband's recovery was unavoidably present in both of her primary systems—home and work—no matter how hard she might try to keep them separate. When pressed, Teresa admitted that even when she did come into the office, part of her was constantly worried about her husband and his struggles.

Teresa Connects the Dots

To stay connected, Bob explained, was about something much more than "keeping up" with things. From a systems perspective, it simply was not realistic to think that Teresa's deep anxiety over her husband's illness could be contained to her family system alone. In effect, Teresa had been emotionally MIA for many months, and it was not surprising that her team had picked up on it at some level—most likely below conscious awareness, but perhaps not entirely. The resistance she had encountered from her people was not deliberate; it was symptomatic of the previous (mostly calm) equilibrium of the emotional system having been disturbed. They were feeling more anxious now, and as a result, they were not as willing to take the risks involved in Teresa's new initiatives—especially in light of her felt absence. Teresa's previous leadership style had been very much hands-on whenever the firm was facing a new challenge. But now, because she was more disconnected in some significant ways, she was not able to exert that positive, calming influence that had always been a key factor in the innovative spirit that characterized her team.

STOP & REFLECT

- **How emotionally present and available have you been to your team in recent weeks?**
- **If you have noticed too much distance on your part, how might you adjust?**

Staying Connected to a Dispersed Workforce

In a world where more and more organizations have workers telecommuting and increasingly dispersed around the globe, leaders are faced with significant challenges as they attempt to stay connected in ways that allow them to exert a positive influence on those they lead. We have collaborated with many leaders who have understood and met the challenges successfully, so we know it is possible. Here are some of the best practices that have helped resilient leaders meet those challenges:

- Establish and maintain a regular routine of calls (audio/video) with stakeholders, both one-on-one and group and commit to making those calls a priority (treat them like important in-person meetings).
- Be mindful and intentional about the quality of your presence. Maintain a centered, less anxious presence and re-center throughout your calls/writing your e-mails as needed.
- Use e-mail not only to coordinate the completion of tasks but to check in with and take the temperature of those remotely located.
- Reinforce clarity in the rational system by communicating key decisions and in general keep connected to people by sharing with them your perspective on the state of the things that matter to them and to you.
- Regularly practice E-Mailing Mindfully. (See the Core Practice at the end of this chapter.)
- Be strategic about making in-person visits where possible, and use that time to connect on the feeling level with as many people as possible.
- Listen and learn about what is going on during visits to remote locations and follow up when you get back home in a way that shows you have truly heard those remote workers and their concerns.
- Handwritten notes, however short, carry a very powerful message, particularly in this age of electronic communications. Consider developing a regular routine of handwriting short notes of appreciation.

Third Big Idea—A New Way of LEADING: Work on maintaining a healthy balance between being close enough to influence yet distant enough to lead.

Teresa's story above provided a good example of how detrimental it can be when a leader does not stay connected closely enough to those she leads. John—the new supervisor we introduced at the start of this chapter—provides a good example of how detrimental it can be when a leader's default tendency leans in the opposite direction, toward fusion. But what does it look like when a leader strikes a healthier balance? Let's pick back up on John's story to see what it reveals about the pitfalls of being too close and the potential for healthier functioning when a leader course corrects.

Despite his misgivings, John continued to attend happy hour every Friday with his former peers (now his employees) and found himself getting caught up in their gossip and complaints about other managers and teams. While he had participated in this kind of workplace banter as a teammate, his comments now struck a different chord as the team leader. In fact, word spread quickly to the other managers and teams in his organization that John was "bad-mouthing" them and taking sides with his employees. Not surprisingly, they began to distance themselves from him at every turn, excluding John on important e-mail chains and "forgetting" to invite him to key meetings.

John was also struggling with the employee who had interviewed for the team-lead position that John now held. Angry that he hadn't been chosen, this employee's performance began to slide, and his attitude worsened. John felt bad for the employee (after all, he had more experience than John and a family to support), and his feelings of guilt kept John from giving him feedback until the situation finally came to a head. Instead of accepting the feedback for what it was, the employee pushed back and accused John of being "uppity."

John himself began to wonder if managing was something he was cut out to do, and he began to have serious doubts about his abilities and his future. Fortunately, John's boss decided to give him the benefit of the doubt and signed John up for some leadership coaching to see if he could overcome his reluctance to lead and recover from his early stumbles. John was eager to learn how he could do better and made the most of his coaching opportunity, much to the delight of his boss.

The heart of the lesson John learned from his coaching was that staying connected in just the right way to those he was leading required him to be **close enough to influence yet distant enough to lead**. He came to realize that leaders can never be just "one of the gang." Close relationships that are perfectly appropriate among peers in social settings can be fatal traps for a leader who does not appreciate the distance required by the position s/he occupies within the organization's rational and emotional systems. Leadership is sometimes a lonely place, and a leader needs to understand that fact and have sufficient interior resources to persevere through those solitary times. The truth of this fact is on vivid display when parents just want to be pals with their children and abdicate responsibility for enforcing appropriate discipline.

Leadership is sometimes a lonely place, and a leader needs to understand that fact and have sufficient interior resources to persevere through those times.

When the Leader Misses the Right Balance

What happens when a leader does not keep the right, healthy close-distant balance is predictable. For the leader, there is a loss of perspective and an inability to be objective about the needs of the system and/or the needs of particular followers. When a leader is too close or too distant, it is impossible to SEE accurately what is happening in the emotional system, and poor judgments about how to manage the rational system inevitably follow. This was true for both John and Teresa.

From the side of those who look to the leader for effective leadership, there is confusion ("Who's in charge here?") and, without clear direction or boundaries from the leader, reactivity increases. The leader's ability to influence followers also erodes the longer the leader is too close or too distant. Every system needs and craves a leader, but when the leader is emotionally MIA due to an inability to strike the proper balance on the close-distant continuum, the leader's moves are at the very least ineffective and generally counterproductive.

John Course Corrects

The ideal, of course, looks quite different, and these are some of the behaviors that John eventually learned and practiced to mastery:

- He no longer sought or needed to be "one of the gang."
- He was able to state his position on issues without worrying if everyone would agree or support him.
- Being popular or even well-liked by his employees was less important to him than doing the right thing.
- He still cared—but not too much—about the emotional reactions of those he was leading. This allowed him to have tough conversations and make difficult decisions, even ones that were unpopular.
- He listened to other viewpoints and was able to compromise or even accept others' views when they were superior to his own.
- He knew how to step in to provide guidance and support, but he also would step out appropriately to let others do their jobs.
- He remained emotionally present and available to those he led, without taking his eye off what was needed to manage the rational system.

STOP & REFLECT

- **Looking at the behaviors above that John learned to master, which of these are strengths of yours right now?**
- **Which of the behaviors above are ones you might adopt and practice in order to strike a better balance between being "close enough to influence, yet distant enough to lead"? What difference might this make in your leadership?**

Staying connected in a healthy way—what we've been calling "close enough to influence yet distant enough to lead"—is always important to effective leadership. However, there are times when pausing to assess the balance you are striking with various stakeholders (your employees, boss, peers, clients, etc.) is particularly important. Such times include when you are promoted into a new role (like John was), or when you are experiencing personal challenges or hardships that demand your attention (like Teresa was). Other situations where we may need to assess and potentially recalibrate our close-distant balance include times of heightened organizational or team change or uncertainty when our presence (both emotionally and physically) can make all the difference in calming an anxious system.

The Pursuit-Distancing Pattern

A last relevant point worth mentioning here is the importance of a leader paying attention to a very commonplace pattern that can easily fly under the radar. A systems perspective always looks for reciprocal dynamics, since that is how every system strives to keep itself in balance. The over/underfunctioning pattern is the most obvious example. But there is also a pursuit-flight pattern that can easily develop when a leader is attempting to move an important organizational agenda forward (or even keep a direct report focused on a priority task that is running behind schedule). The reciprocal nature of all relationships guarantees that whenever a leader is in pursuit of another person or group—especially when his/her pursuit is characterized by a high degree of emotional intensity—the person (or group) automatically and instinctively begins to flee. Because this instinctive reaction operates below conscious awareness, the one(s) being pursued may be completely unaware of their distancing, ignoring, or otherwise resisting the overtures of the one who is pursuing.

How many parents have quickly learned the lesson that their toddler will gleefully run away just when the parent is most eager to corral him/her at dinnertime? Instead of investing the time required to play this game that the child delights in, the shrewd parent will feign disinterest and seem to walk in the opposite direction, trusting that the child will make an about-face and follow the parent with curiosity once there no longer seems to be a pursuit. In our adult version of this pattern, we generally urge leaders to stop chasing after the delinquent person or group when the leader's repeated efforts have been fruitless. As long as there are accountability measures in place that keep the responsibility (and the consequences) for a failure to meet deadlines on the delinquent one(s), it is a best practice for the leader to step back and stop fueling the reciprocal dynamic with escalating intensity (aka anxiety) in the form of continuing reminders (or demands).

Core Practices

Be Separate yet Stay Connected

Pick a colleague or family member with whom you want to be more intentional about striking a healthy balance between distance and closeness. Thoughtfully consider what steps you might take to bridge too much distance if that is the case, or to course correct if there is too much closeness. Before, during, and after interactions with this person, regularly assess how you're doing.

E-Mail Mindfully

Remember that once an e-mail is sent, it cannot be unsent.

Compose the draft e-mail.

Stop and take one long, deep breath. Pay attention to the breath. You can count to five on the inhale and again on the exhale if you like. Repeat two or three times.

Think of the person to whom the e-mail is going and how you want her/him to receive your message. Could s/he misunderstand your words and become angry or offended, or think you're being more positive or negative than you intend? Get in touch with what you are feeling underneath the words you are using.

Decide if the e-mail is mostly transactional, needs immediate attention, and requires that you complete it in one sitting. If the content and character of the e-mail is more transformational and must be "just right," put the assignment away for a time and return to the note later with a fresh perspective.

Look at the draft e-mail again and revise if necessary before hitting send.

Chapter Summary

- All human beings strive to balance two forces deeply embedded within them—the need to be a separate self and the need to form close connections with others. How well we manage these fundamental drives determines the health of our relationships and our organizations.
- A leader can only exert a positive influence on a system to which he or she is connected.
- When anxiety rises in our relationship systems, we each have a default tendency we favor—either toward too much closeness (fusion) or too much distance (cutoff). Either extreme results in a loss of influence.
- Leaders who are either too close or too distant from those they lead provoke anxiety and reactivity in others. Either extreme makes people wonder at some level, "Who's in charge here?"
- Resilient leaders are aware of their default tendency and work to strike a better balance when needed between being "close enough to influence yet distant enough to lead."
- Good organizational health, like good individual health, is related to how well members strike a balance between too much togetherness (reflected in groupthink, herding, and excessive water-cooler gossip) or too much distance (reflected in closed doors, hiding out in offices, or excessive absences).
- A resilient leader will notice when her/his family, team, or organization is moving toward too much distance or too much closeness and will take steps to restore a better balance. S/he will draw out those who are disengaged and too distant, or encourage those who are too close to step back and take some time apart to avoid fueling others' anxieties.

CHAPTER 5

BALANCE THE SEESAW
Avoid Overfunctioning and Improve Underperformance

> We co-create each other. We are constantly emerging out of the relationship we have with others.
>
> —Ruth Ozeki

You might recall that in Chapter 1, we suggested that a resilient leader is well-equipped to deal with a VUCA world. Again, that acronym stands for "volatility, uncertainty, complexity, and ambiguity." The clients we work with often tell us that VUCA is an apt description of today's workplace. Many of them are doing their best to survive in their high-stress, fast-paced, and complex work environments, but most want to do more than just survive. Rather, they aspire to thrive and to create workplaces in which their employees can thrive as well.

The topic that we turn our attention to in this chapter—over- and underfunctioning—is key both to surviving and thriving in a VUCA world, where committed, conscientious leaders often burn out themselves and / or the people they lead. To understand why, let's start with the definition of *overfunctioning,* which is "to think, feel, or act for another in a way that erodes another's capacity for ownership or thoughtful action."

Notice that overfunctioning is not just about doing for others; it includes thinking or feeling for others in a way that interferes with their own self-efficacy. This means that excessive worrying is a form of overfunctioning, as is spending too much time thinking about how to solve another's problem.

To over-function means to think, feel, or act for another, in a way that erodes their capacity for ownership or thoughtful action.

As we unpack our definition of overfunctioning, we begin to see that burnout is not simply a rational-world, quantitative issue—a matter of working too long or putting in too many hours; rather, it is largely an emotional-world phenomenon, created by feeling responsible for things that are not ours to carry. The solution, therefore, is not necessarily to do less (although that is often part of it), but rather *to feel less responsible* for what is another's responsibility to own.

What's at Stake Here?

The COO of a large nonprofit that Bob and Bridgette worked with on a change-management project once said to them, "Why should I care if my staff overfunctions? They're mission-driven, and I get more bang for my buck out of them!" He said this half-jokingly, but underneath his remark was a genuine desire to understand why we had raised the issue as one deserving of his attention. His flip comment opened up a valuable conversation, and we were able to identify with him some of the reasons why the overfunctioning of his key leaders needed to be a matter of concern for him. Briefly, we pointed out—and he came to realize—that overfunctioning comes with a high price.

Consequences of Overfunctioning

- **Failure to scale.** Organizations may be able to do a successful "sprint" by asking leaders and others to go after a short-term stretch goal, but in the long run, an organization that is interested in elevating its operations to reach a new level of performance simply cannot build on a foundation of overfunctioning. Jim Collins uses a flywheel analogy in his famous book *Good to Great* to describe how well-run companies produce and sustain high performance. He recounts several examples where companies slowly and carefully build their capacity and capability to compete and win in their marketplace. Collins's point is that successful company "flywheels" pick up speed gradually, incrementally, not as a result of short bursts of overfunctioning, but rather with sustained, ongoing development of capability and capacity.

- **Burnout**. We describe resilient leaders as those who "lead from strength, know how to care for themselves emotionally, spiritually and physically, and can sustain their leadership efforts over time." By definition, sustainability is key to long-term success, and the most resilient leaders are those who have learned to pace themselves at just the right speed over the long haul. The effects of a leader's burnout can be devastating, and unfortunately, most organizations have many stories of the way a leader's burnout has been a dead weight—or worse—on the organization at large.

- **Poor health**. Prolonged overfunctioning translates into a sustained stress response, which results in our bodies being overexposed to cortisol, adrenaline, and other stress hormones—all of which disrupt normal bodily functioning. Accumulating research studies have documented the increased risk of health problems that result, including:
    - Anxiety
    - Depression
    - Digestive problems
    - Headaches
    - Heart disease
    - Sleep problems
    - Weight gain
    - Memory and concentration impairment

STOP & REFLECT

- **As you consider your various relationship systems at work and at home, where and with whom might you be overfunctioning?**
- **To the extent that you (or other members of your team) are overfunctioning, what is the impact on you? On the people around you? On the system as a whole?**

First Big Idea—A New Way of SEEING: Observe the role anxiety plays in your own over/underfunctioning.

Is It Always Overfunctioning?

We were doing Resilient Leadership training for a client some years ago, and during the discussion of overfunctioning, one of the participants raised a very helpful point: "My team and I work very hard, and we regularly outperform our goals, offer to take on special projects even though we are all busy, stay late if the job requires it, and in general do more than is asked or expected of us. Does that mean we are all overfunctioning?"

Our answer to her was a cautious one. "It depends," we said. "To what extent do you think your very strong work ethic is driven by anxiety, and are you energized—rather than exhausted—by being a high-performing team?"

She already understood what we meant by anxiety in this context, so we did not have to explain that we were referencing the fuller notion of chronic anxiety that we explored in Chapter 2, where we described reactivity as the public face of anxiety. What she also understood is that chronic anxiety is neither healthy nor toxic in itself and that the answer to our "it depends" was a way of asking her to get in touch with how much chronic anxiety was present in her, her team, and in the larger work system of which they were parts.

Stress is not the same thing as anxiety. We can nearly always recognize our stressors but chronic anxiety operates at a level too deep for direct observation.

The conversation that followed was rich. We talked about the fact that anxiety is not the same thing as the stress that comes from having a great deal of work to do. If we stop to think about it, we can nearly always recognize our stressors (for example, a demanding boss, impossible deadlines, a critical lack of resources, and so forth) and we can usually measure how much stress we are under as a result. What is not so easy to recognize is the degree of chronic anxiety that is churning within us and within the relationship systems we are part of at work and at home. Chronic anxiety operates at a level too deep for direct observation because it is part of our instinctive, automatic functioning.

As a result, we acknowledged that it was very tricky to sort out whether the work ethic of this team was a form of reactive functioning or an admirable and healthy example of a high-performing team. One way to make an assessment, we suggested, would be to consider the definition of overfunctioning ("to think, feel, or act for another in a way that erodes one's capacity for ownership and effective action") and then to look for objective signs that this is or is not happening. Most of us overfunction because it works for us—in the short term. We overfunction because it helps us to offload some of the anxiety we are feeling about a particular relationship or situation. But then we continue to overfunction, because we no longer see another way to alleviate anxiety. At that point, overfunctioning can become an addictive process rather than an occasional aberration.

How Our Stories Fuel Overfunctioning

Another way to discern whether we are anxiously overfunctioning is to listen to the story we are telling ourselves about why we must overfunction and the consequences that we assume will occur if we fail to do so. One of our expert RL coaches shared a personal story about her pattern of overfunctioning for her teenage son that was both humorous and revealing. He was having difficulty getting up in the morning and making it to school on time, despite the fact that he was in high school and should have been able to accomplish that task without her aid. After several days of him being late to school, she found herself "helping" him in a myriad of ways, first by waking him up when he ignored his alarm clock, then knocking on the bathroom door several times when he was spending too much time in the shower, and finally even by buttering his toast for him so he could eat a quicker breakfast!

The turning point came when her husband said to her one morning, "How long are you going to butter this kid's toast for him and get him out of the shower?" At that moment, she realized the full extent of her overfunctioning and became curious as to what was driving it. Upon reflection, she came to see that she was incredibly anxious about her son making it to school on time because if he didn't, he would "fail at life and never become a full-fledged, contributing member of society!" Of course, this was a story she had made up in her head, one that provoked a great deal of anxiety within her (and within him, no doubt), and in turn, led her to overfunctioning. Only when she stepped back to thoughtfully consider what was driving her behavior and the impact it was having on her son could she begin to unravel the pattern and step out of it.

STOP & REFLECT

- **See if you can get in touch with the story you are telling yourself about why you must overfunction in a particular situation:**
- **What are the "untenable" consequences you fear might happen if you were to stop?**
- **To what extent are your assumptions true?**

Second Big Idea—A New Way of THINKING: Understand the reciprocal nature of over/underfunctioning.

Bridgette was asked to coach Sara—a bright but somewhat insecure recent hire at a tech firm—by her boss, Jim (also a recent hire), who was concerned about Sara's frequent failure to delegate effectively to the members of the two teams she was leading. Jim was also increasingly annoyed by Sara's frantic pace and by the way she kept hijacking their conversations, peppering him with a dozen problems and demands every time they talked.

Sara welcomed the opportunity to work with a coach, and Bridgette found her remarkably open and eager to understand how she could show up in her new job as a high performer. Over the next few months, Bridgette was able to observe firsthand that Sara was both overfunctioning and underfunctioning. With her teams, she over-talked, over-explained, and then over-managed, even though all of the team members were bright and highly qualified in their roles. And, Sara's tendency to take on tasks that she should have delegated meant that she was falling behind in many of the responsibilities that were uniquely hers—something Jim had observed with growing concern.

What's Going On Here?

Bridgette also learned that as part of the senior team, Sara was anxiously underperforming. In the bimonthly meetings with her peers and several senior leaders, Sara kept such a low profile that she was almost invisible when matters of substance were being discussed. Sara acknowledged to Bridgette that she was aware of how frequently she "shut down" in those meetings, fearful that if she asserted herself and made a misstep, it could derail her hopes of advancement. Bridgette was also beginning to pick up on the fact that Jim was underfunctioning in his relationship to Sara, withdrawing from her when he was annoyed by her overfunctioning and increasingly turning to her peers rather than to her when he needed help on a project. This in turn only made Sara more anxious and even less likely to speak up during the senior-team meetings and assert herself as he expected and wanted her to.

While Jim was clear about the potential impact of Sara's failure to delegate, what he was less clear about was his own contribution to the anxious reactivity that swirled around both of them. Like Jim, many of the leaders we work with can often spot over- or underfunctioning in others but have more difficulty seeing their own role in the reciprocal pattern.

Thinking Systems

The New Way of THINKING described in the Resilient Leadership model suggests that leaders must *think systems* to understand more fully the complex dynamics of the network of relationships (aka the emotional systems) they lead. This kind of thinking does not come naturally, and it is only after a prolonged and sustained effort that we can strengthen our mental muscles in that direction. The reason it takes time and effort to develop the ability to think systems is that our brains are hardwired for a simpler, more direct cause-effect way of thinking: someone or something does A, and that causes B to happen, which in turn causes C, and that leads to D—and so forth. This is what is called *linear thinking* rather than *systems thinking*.

A resilient leader will be on the alert for how what is happening in the larger system may be influencing a specific part of the organization.

Systems thinking, on the other hand, encompasses the connections between both recurring patterns and random, seemingly unconnected events in the multiple interactions that occur throughout the entire relationship network. A resilient leader will look for reciprocal influences underlying those events, even when the direct connections are not obvious. Such a leader will also be on the alert for how what is happening in the larger emotional system(s) may be influencing a specific part of the organization.

Thinking systems is like moving from a microscope to a wide-angle lens. A systems thinker is concerned with gathering the facts (what, where, when, etc.), not with asking why. When a specific symptom surfaces, the leader who thinks systems approaches the symptom not just as a problem to solve but as a window from which to observe how the larger system is functioning. (It's complicated!) And since the dynamics of an emotional system operate at a deep level—most often beneath conscious awareness and not directly observable—thinking systems is never a precise or quantifiable science. (It's very complicated indeed!)

Foundational Principles

The good news, however, is that there are some solid, foundational principles that can guide our understanding of so much complexity. Doing systems thinking well is akin to an art form where intuition and insight blend with structural rules, allowing a leader to recognize and understand patterns, nuanced clues, and marker events in a way that provides deeper understanding, not just hints or suspicions.

The reciprocal nature of the over/underfunctioning dynamic is one of those foundational principles that allows us to "think systems" in a way that can often connect the dots between apparently disparate parts of the system. Because an emotional system operates more as a force field than a machine, we understand that even a relatively minor input by a leader can reverberate at the furthest reaches of the system, often at a speed that amazes even the most seasoned leader.

Sara, whom we met above, manifested her anxiety by overfunctioning with her team and pursuing Jim, her boss, with a barrage of questions and problems every time they were together. We also noted that Jim was a relatively new hire and was likewise anxious about looking good to his superiors and was increasingly concerned about Sara's performance, lest his decision to hire her be seen as a shortcoming on his part.

Two things we know for certain: (1) over / underfunctioning is always anxiety-driven; and (2) over / underfunctioning is always a reciprocal phenomenon. Sara's overfunctioning manifested itself in multiple contexts, and the reciprocal dynamics likewise appeared in multiple venues. Jim was new in his job and was anxious about looking good, and it is not hard to understand why a chronic overfunctioner like Sara would have become a subject of anxious focus for him quite quickly. Her anxiety was intense and contagious, and because she was usually unaware of it, she had little capacity to manage it. In her mind, the way she was pursuing Jim was legitimate, given that she was new on the job and he was her supervisor. When he began to underfunction by avoiding her, it only served to raise her anxiety and increase her pursuit. The more she pursued, the more he made himself unavailable.

Two things we know for certain: (1) Over/under-functioning is always anxiety-driven. (2) Over/under-functioning is always a reciprocal phenomenon.

Underfunctioning in Our Personal Lives

From Bridgette's perspective, she also saw that Sara was underfunctioning not only in the senior team but in another very important relationship: with herself. It is nearly always the case that when a person is overfunctioning in one sphere of life, s/he is underfunctioning in some other sphere(s), quite often with health or personal relationships with family and friends. Early on in their coaching relationship, Sara told Bridgette that since she had taken her new job, she had dropped her long-standing commitment to an exercise routine and had gained nearly twenty pounds. As a single mother, she had long ago learned the importance of a support system of other young moms, neighbors, and friends who could step in as a safety net when the demands of work limited her availability and she needed help with her kids. But in recent months, she had had little time to connect (or to reciprocate) with the people in that network, and a growing isolation was the result.

STOP & REFLECT

- **If you are overfunctioning in your leadership role, there is underfunctioning somewhere in the system you lead.**
- **Who might be underfunctioning in response to you?**
- **What is the impact of their diminished functioning on them? And on you? And on the system?**

Third Big Idea—A New Way of LEADING: Act to break the cycle by focusing on your own functioning.

Both over- and underfunctioning can easily become addictive processes that operate much like addictive substances that promise to alleviate our pain—physical or psychological—but come with a very, very high price. Both over- and underfunctioning are fueled by a high level of anxiety, and we recall that anxiety is nature's automatic response in the face of a perceived threat. None of us feels comfortable or good under threat—and particularly when the anxiety is abiding (chronic anxiety), we instinctively want relief from it. The higher the anxiety and the longer we must bear

it, the greater the urgency we feel to be free of the threat.
The nature of the perceived threats that generate higher-than-comfortable levels of anxiety are as varied as the diversity of humankind itself. So, too, are the manifestations of over- and underfunctioning. Because our brain always wants to justify and make sense out of the automatic functioning that holds us in its grip, we rationalize why this or that form of anxious functioning makes perfect sense and is meaningful and even necessary. The reasons we invent to convince ourselves that we cannot—must not—give up the comfort of the addictive process are nearly inexhaustible. Consider how ingenious are the varied disguises that over- and underfunctioning wear:

Manifestations of Overfunctioning

- Worrying too much about someone else
- Doing work that you can and should delegate to others
- Thinking you know what is best for someone else
- Offering advice before it's asked for
- Expecting others to do it your way
- Taking over someone else's job without being asked
- Feeling responsible for someone else's feelings
- Correcting someone else's work without telling them about it

Manifestations of Underfunctioning

- Not making decisions
- Constantly seeking advice
- Habitually letting others have their way
- Not taking initiative
- Adopting a weak or helpless persona
- Believing others are responsible for your feelings
- Not speaking up and sharing your point of view
- Resigning yourself to the idea that "it's hopeless"

STOP & REFLECT

- **As you look at the behaviors associated with overfunctioning that we have listed above, which ones can you see in yourself? When and with whom do you exhibit this behavior?**
- **As you look at the behaviors associated with underfunctioning, to what extent do you recognize any of them in your own functioning? When and with whom do you exhibit this behavior?**

Sometimes the patterns of over- or underfunctioning that we've adopted to calm our anxious fears become the daily background of the lives we lead, and this familiarity makes us come to see them as normal and "just who I am." But some patterns are more progressive than chronic, and so more and more energy is required to keep at bay our escalating levels of anxiety. Our coping mechanisms become as burdensome as the anxiety itself, and we can come to a point where we either crash and burn or reach out for help to rescue us from the death spiral.

Sara's Awakening

The solid coaching relationship that Bridgette had built with Sara in the story we shared earlier made it possible for her to support Sara as she came to realize what was at stake in her over- and underfunctioning patterns and decided to take steps to rebalance her life.

At first, Sara was fairly unaware of the nature and extent of her over- and underfunctioning. Then, in a coaching session, she told Bridgette how burdened she felt because she "had to" do so much of the work that her team should have been doing. Bridgette shared with her our definitions of over- and underfunctioning as given above and simply asked her to observe and keep track of whether she saw any of that in herself.

Sara's response at their next coaching session was a much clearer recognition of the fact and the extent of her anxiety-driven behaviors but also an admission that she felt helpless to turn her life around. Bridgette pointed out that her reactive functioning was in great measure automatic and without conscious awareness, whereas the road to recovery was in the direction of a more self-aware and more thoughtful pattern of functioning. Acting to break the cycle must be done from a calm and clear place, not a reactionary one.

Bridgette also cautioned Sara that breaking the cycle is neither easy nor quick, and along the path to recovery, many obstacles would be sure to surface. For example, many apparent benefits often come to those who overfunction. In many systems, it is those who overfunction who are rewarded with promotions and other recognitions. Being willing to forgo such rewards (in status, favor, etc.) might be something we have to face as part of breaking the cycle.

STOP & REFLECT

- **To what extent is overfunctioning rewarded in your system?**
- **What are the "rewards" for overfunctioning?**
- **What happens to those who consistently underfunction?**

Another potential pitfall along the path to recovery is that often when a person stops overfunctioning, those who have been involved with them in a reciprocal pattern of underfunctioning actually underfunction to an even greater degree before they begin to rebalance their functioning in a better way.

Martin's Awakening

Bob once coached a very senior leader, Martin, whose responsibility it was to finalize policy issues that carried enormous financial consequences for a global company. Martin's staff often gave him "final" drafts that needed more work. After a number of tries to get his team to do a better job in preparing work for the CEO's signature, he had fallen into a pattern of revising and finalizing documents himself, most often on weekends or late into the evening. Because of the potential costs of a misstep, he was unwilling to give the CEO anything less than a perfect document for his signature.

Bob helped Martin realize that his anxiety over making a "fatal mistake" (his words) had led him to treat every single document as if it carried ultimate consequences and required perfection in content, style, and even formatting! As he learned how to focus on his own anxious functioning in a more thoughtful way, Martin could see that not everything was of ultimate importance, and he had to be much more discriminating about when circumstances truly required him to refine the language of a "final" draft, what should be passed back to his team for further work, and what could be sent up to the CEO or other stakeholders as is despite being less polished than he would have wished.

STOP & REFLECT

- **What might be possible for me, my team, or my organization if I stopped over- or underfunctioning?**

With Bob's help, Martin drew up a list of questions that he would ask himself in various situations when he was trying to figure out if he was being tempted to overfunction. By way of example, here are a few of them:

- Do I need to better define roles, responsibilities, or expectations?
- Is what I'm doing anxiety driven?
- What am I responsible for in this situation? What are others responsible for?
- Am I taking action that will discourage others from owning or doing the work they are responsible for?
- If I don't break the cycle, what are the likely consequences?

Over time, Martin's anxiety subsided as he saw more objectively that good enough is most often truly just that—good enough—and did not require him to make it better. As Bob had warned him, when he stopped revising the work of his team, their initial response was to become even more careless in some of the documents they forwarded to him. But when they eventually realized that he was likely to pass on their work to the CEO as is, the quality of the products they sent up to him significantly improved. At that point, Martin also began thoughtfully, not reactively, to raise the bar with his team in several other respects. Much to his delight, what soon became clear to him was that his overfunctioning had been inhibiting the talented people around him from performing at their best.

Often, people who are working on better management of their over- or underfunctioning behaviors wonder if they need to give those around them a heads-up about their efforts to break the cycle. In general, this is not necessary, since in an emotional system, others will adjust their behaviors to the change automatically, usually without consciously recognizing what has happened. Our focus should be squarely on what we are going to *start* doing or *stop* doing, not on what or whom we need to tell about our intent. One exception might be when it seems helpful to get the support of a trusted colleague who can observe our behavior up close and give us ongoing feedback about our slips and our progress as we work over time to change deeply ingrained patterns.

Sara: The Rest of the Story

We bring this chapter to a conclusion by sharing the rest of the story of the slow but steady progress Sara made in her efforts to focus on and lower her anxiety-driven behaviors. Bridgette coached her on how to speak up more forcefully and substantively in the senior-team meetings, much to Jim's delight. Because she was learning to pay more attention to the emotional dynamics in the room, she was able to recognize that when she did speak up, others listened attentively and frequently telegraphed approval in their body language, if not by explicit comments. This in turn helped her to stop underfunctioning and become more engaged in the important conversations shared at the senior-team level.

Bridgette also helped Sara to yield more responsibility for significant projects to the members of her teams. They in turn did not disappoint her; they delighted her with the expertise and proficiency with which they exceeded her expectations. The virtuous circle of successful delegation followed by successful performance that resulted further lowered Sara's anxiety and lessened her micromanaging behaviors.

When Bridgette's coaching engagement concluded, Sara was still a work in progress, and from time to time she relapsed into old patterns. However, she had made significant progress in self-awareness and had learned to manage her anxious behaviors by using several core practices to calm herself and keep her focus on her own functioning. Jim reported that he considered the coaching a success, and Bridgette's observation was that he too displayed fewer anxious-behavior patterns than before. The system at large had calmed down due to the focused efforts of two of its key leaders, and the frequency of over/underfunctioning behaviors was noticeably reduced in Sara and the members of her team.

> **Sara had made significant progress in self-awareness and had learned to manage her anxious behaviors by using several "core practices" to calm herself and keep her focus on her own functioning.**

Core Practices

Balance the Seesaw If You Are Overfunctioning

1. Next time you find yourself *thinking, feeling, or acting for another*, pause and ask yourself:
   - How can I be a resource in this situation without taking it all on?
   - How might my overfunctioning be eroding the other's capacity for ownership or effective action?
2. Adjust your functioning and trust the reciprocal nature of the system to rebalance the other side.

Balance the Seesaw If You Are Underfunctioning

1. Next time you find yourself *allowing the behavior of others to diminish your functioning*, pause and ask yourself:
   - To what extent am I taking responsibility for my underfunctioning versus blaming others?
   - How might I show up in this situation as a clearer, more well-defined *self*?
2. Adjust your functioning and trust the reciprocal nature of the system to rebalance the other side.

Chapter Summary

- *Overfunctioning* means "to think, feel or act for another in a way that erodes their capacity for ownership and effective action." From this perspective, even excessive worrying is a form of overfunctioning.
- *Underfunctioning* is "allowing the behavior of others to diminish one's own functioning."
- The impact of over/underfunctioning is significant and has both personal and organizational costs, including increased burnout, failure to elevate performance, and erosion of employee engagement and development.
- Over/underfunctioning is a form of reactivity and is driven by the anxiety we feel in a relationship system. Getting in touch with this anxiety is a key part of untangling ourselves from the pattern.
- The good news? You can change the over/underfunctioning seesaw that you are on by focusing on your own functioning. The other side will adjust in response without you having to coax or will it to change.
- All over/underfunctioning is supported and held in place by an underlying narrative or story. Listen for the story you are telling yourself and/or others about why you must over- or underfunction, and be curious about the assumptions underlying your story.
- Entire departments or teams can engage in the over/underfunctioning pattern. If you manage such a department or team, focus on helping your employees to see how they are contributing to the pattern, and explore together how you might collectively reduce anxiety and change the team's functioning in a thoughtful and deliberate way.
- Over/underfunctioning is always a reciprocal pattern, like a seesaw: you can't have one without the other. If you are over- or underfunctioning regularly at work and/or home, the reciprocal is happening somewhere in the system.

CHAPTER 6

MANAGE TRIANGLES
LOWER YOUR STRESS AND IMPROVE YOUR HEALTH AND EFFECTIVENESS

Almost every issue of leadership and the difficulties that accompany it can be framed in terms of emotional triangles including motivation, clarity, decision-making, resistance to change, imaginative gridlock and a failure of nerve.

—Edwin Friedman
A Failure of Nerve

Remember from Chapter 4 the story about Bridgette's son at age five and his impassioned declaration, *"I need to be my own person"*? Skip forward ten years: the same young man was now reasserting his independence as an adolescent.

Sam and his father, Doug, had always enjoyed a good, solid relationship. But at age fifteen, Sam was beginning to test and renegotiate that relationship by asserting his growing independence in many of the ways that teens typically do. The result was a good bit of reactivity between father and son as each triggered the other. Over a period of months, there were more and more times when friction between them developed and a clash of wills ensued.

Not surprisingly, both of them would seek out Bridgette to complain about the other and to gain her support for their side of the story. Caring deeply for both of them, she sought to de-escalate the tensions between them, sometimes by offering advice (often unsolicited), sometimes by serving as an intermediary trying to broker a solution acceptable to both of them and sometimes thinking one or the other might not have handled his part of the situation very well. None of her efforts seemed to help, and her anxiety about the conflict between the two grew.

What's Going On Here?

Bridgette was, of course, caught in a classic family triangle. Sam was their firstborn, and as young parents, this was Doug and Bridgette's first experience managing the emotional roller coaster of adolescence. The situation had not escalated in any dramatic fashion, and Sam's rebellious behaviors were fairly modest. But Bridgette felt herself caught in the middle and was torn in her loyalties time and again. She became anxious over the way the wonderful relationship between father and son had deteriorated, and she was routinely distracted with thoughts about how she could restore the harmony between them.

In what seemed at the time to Bridgette like an act of divine providence, this period coincided precisely with her introduction to the work of Ed Friedman and his explanation of the laws of emotional triangles. In the pages that follow, we will share with you some of the insights that allowed Bridgette to reposition herself in the family triangle in a way that lessened her stress and opened up new possibilities for Sam and Doug to work through the bumpy spots in their relationship in better ways.

The emotional systems of families and organizations operate according to the same principles.

Because the emotional systems of families and organizations operate according to the same principles, you will see that these insights and practices of managing triangles are applicable in both places—at home and at work. You will also learn that once leaders understand triangles and manage themselves differently in them, their stress lowers, their health improves, and their effectiveness increases.

First Big Idea—A New Way of SEEING: Observe that triangles are nature's way of lowering anxiety, and they are everywhere!

By now, you surely know that in the First Big Idea, we always try to demonstrate how important it is for a leader to become more skilled at observing the dynamics of the emotional system. The phrase *emotional system* is a shorthand way of describing the instinctive, automatic interactions that characterize every network of relationships. The term *chronic anxiety* also captures the energy field that makes those relationships so dynamic and ever-shifting, as every segment of the system is always attempting to strike a healthy balance in the face of perceived threats that inevitably arise in a constantly changing environment.

We have also stressed that the energy field that makes up the emotional system is invisible and lies beneath our conscious awareness. It is the hidden chemistry of every organization and every family. For that reason, it is reactivity—the public face of anxiety—that we encourage a leader to recognize and observe in all of its diverse manifestations. Previous chapters have pointed out some of the different forms that reactivity takes, and we have suggested that leaders should work at becoming more skilled in recognizing the presence of reactivity in self, in others, and in the larger system. We have explored some of these classic examples of reactivity:

- A presence that is more anxious than others and so increases, rather than calms, their anxiety
- Relationships that are characterized by too much closeness or too much distance
- A loss of self that is revealed when leaders have no clear vision or guiding principles of their own
- Leaders who perpetually seek to please others, to avoid conflict, or to imitate the example of those deemed more powerful or more popular
- Over/underfunctioning behaviors that are anxiety driven and that cause others to under/overfunction

All of these expressions of reactivity are sure signs that the level of chronic anxiety within the emotional system is higher than is desirable. Recognizing the role that reactivity plays in forming and perpetuating an emotional triangle—and understanding the laws according to which such triangles work—is yet another way that leaders can enhance their leadership effectiveness. When Bridgette came to understand more about how emotional triangles work, she was able to manage her own reactivity in a much better way, and in so doing, she contributed to a less anxious family system in which Doug and Sam found it easier to negotiate their relationship on their own terms.

The Basic Building Blocks of Every Emotional System

The first thing Bridgette learned was that triangles are the basic building blocks of every emotional system. They are a natural phenomenon, and they are everywhere! It was the research of Murray Bowen into family systems that allowed him to discover the counterintuitive truth that the basic unit of all emotional systems is the triad, not the dyad. He discovered this by careful observation that any twosome quickly and inevitably experiences a sufficient level of anxiety in their relationship that they seek relief by "triangulating in" another person. Both Doug and Sam instinctively sought out Bridgette as a way to alleviate the stress they were feeling in their relationship with each other, and they tried to triangle her into agreeing that they were in the right and the other was at fault. Until she learned about how triangles work, she felt torn between the two.

When leaders first learn about triangles, their initial impulse is often to try to avoid them altogether, since many of them are unhealthy and create more rather than less stress. But it's important to emphasize here that triangles are inevitable (they are the foundation, after all, of every relationship system), and we can't avoid being part of them either at home or at work. What we can do, as we will see in the pages that follow, is determine which ones are toxic, and ultimately reposition ourselves in those triangles to promote healthier functioning.

STOP & REFLECT

- **Are you part of any triangles on the home front that are characterized by high anxiety and tension? If so, are you feeling pressure to take another's side, or are you exerting pressure on others to agree with and take your side?**

- **Are you part of any triangles at work that are characterized by high anxiety and tension? To what extent are you feeling pressure to take sides? To what extent, if at all, are you pressuring others to agree with and take your side?**

Second Big Idea—A New Way of THINKING: Understand the difference between a toxic and a healthy triangle.

> **A triangle is a triad between three people, formed to lower the stress being experienced between two of the people.**

Cheryl was in a heavily matrixed organization, and she was responsible for supporting the work of two leaders of high-performing divisions on a project that was crucial to the organization's success. Both leaders were self-starters and ran their divisions very effectively, but neither of them was particularly good at collaborating with others across disciplines. Cheryl had fallen into the trap of feeling overly responsible for getting them to work together more closely at the level of detail that she knew was essential to integrate their work smoothly into the overall effort. Because the stakes were so high, her anxiety had spiked, and at their first coaching session, she brought to Bob the urgent question: "How can I get them to work together more closely?"

After reviewing whether or not detailed expectations about the project had been clearly communicated to both leaders, Bob shared with Cheryl some basic ideas about how emotional triangles are formed out of anxiety and how they are designed to alleviate the stress felt when anxiety escalates in a system. To her credit, Cheryl was able to recognize that her anxiety had gotten in the way of the two leaders working out the details they needed to manage in order to coordinate their work.

She had bounced from one of them to the other, each time unwittingly escalating anxiety by pointing to the absent leader as not holding up his end of the project and encouraging the leader she was with to take steps to get the project back on schedule. When that person reassured her that he would take action to get things back on track, her stress would temporarily subside. But all that she had done, in reality, was make both leaders more anxious, hooking them into a blaming mindset and making it more difficult for them to work together smoothly. Over several coaching sessions, she came to understand that it was her anxiety that was getting in their way. She very quickly course-corrected and stepped back so they could do what they needed to meet the project deadline.

Cheryl came to realize why reactive triangles form and what happens when anxiety travels around the triangle from person to person. She also realized how quickly reactive blaming can escalate the situation and make it even more difficult to sort out everyday problems. Bob helped her to see how easily and naturally this phenomenon occurs, and how a leader who understands what is happening can take steps to manage the situation (and self) in better (more self-differentiating) ways that promote a calmer, more thoughtful system.

Bob also helped Cheryl understand that not all triangles are unhealthy. Triangles are simply a fact of nature, not a liability to be avoided. It is how one manages self in a triangle that makes it healthy or toxic. There are very clear signs that can alert a perceptive leader to the quality of any triangle. When a triangle is healthy, it lowers anxiety among all three persons involved. People in a healthy triangle tend to think more clearly, and their behaviors are more intentional than automatic and reactive. There is also an openness in a healthy triangle that allows the members to explore richer possibilities in the relationship and to act in more innovative and creative ways.

How Toxic Triangles Work

A toxic triangle, on the other hand, tends to escalate anxiety and promote reactive behaviors. In a toxic triangle, people tend to get stuck in old feeling-driven patterns of thinking, relating, and behaving. In a system, toxic triangles are rarely limited to the original triad; the anxiety they are meant to contain when they first form generally spills over and generates other, interlocking triangles that raise anxiety in the larger organization. Leaders who are caught in anxious triangles frequently have trouble thinking clearly and are prone to distorted perceptions of what is happening in the system. As a result, their ability to take decisive action when it is most needed is also often impaired due to a failure of thoughtfulness, objectivity, imagination, or nerve.

These clues allowed Cheryl to reflect on a number of other important work triangles and to focus on managing herself better in the ones that appeared somewhat toxic, as well as on celebrating and leveraging the healthy ones. One of the triangles Cheryl discussed with Bob included Sandy, a junior member of the organization whom she mentored as part of the organization's leadership-development program. Sandy worked for a bright but demanding—and somewhat scattered—boss. Adjusting to his idiosyncrasies involved considerable stress for Sandy, and she would often vent to Cheryl her frustrations.

Cheryl learned to recognize the difference when her mentoring conversations with Sandy were promoting a healthy or an unhealthy triangle with Sandy and her boss. When Sandy complained about this or that behavior of her boss, it had been easy for Cheryl to slip into commiserating with her, agreeing that the boss tended to be insensitive to women's issues and was known in the organization for failing to meet deadlines. Conversations like that often created a feeling of closeness between Sandy and Cheryl, but they also left Cheryl feeling a bit unsettled.

As she learned about toxic triangles, Cheryl was less and less comfortable with how she had been handling such conversations. She started to work on assuming a more neutral, listening stance and avoided adding any judgmental comments about the boss. Instead, she would sometimes offer advice about how she had found creative ways to work with challenging bosses, or she would ask Sandy questions from a place of curiosity, such as, "Can you think of any other response you might have made that would have left you feeling more empowered rather than like a victim?" Over a period of months, Cheryl noticed that Sandy was becoming less reactive toward her boss, and, from what Cheryl was able to gather, the boss was starting to interact with Sandy in more helpful ways. Just as interlocking triangles that are toxic promote anxiety in the larger system, healthy triangles tend to foster calmer, less reactive systems.

Staying Out of Fix-it Mode

There is one other common mistake that Cheryl was making—exactly the same mistake that Bridgette had made with Doug and Sam before she learned about the laws of triangles. Leaders care about their employees, just as parents care about their children. When two employees (or two family members) are struggling to get along, a leader's (or a parent's) first instinct is to intervene and try to fix whatever may be causing the conflict.

Two of Cheryl's team members—both her direct reports—were constantly at odds with each other. The root cause of their problems was that they had different work styles, but they needed to collaborate closely on projects given to the team. One was a procrastinator, while the other was quick out of the gate and wanted to get any task done as soon as it landed on her desk. Each of them regularly stopped by Cheryl's office to complain about the other, and the longer this went on, the more responsible Cheryl felt to come up with a solution to their problems. She attempted to broker compromises, offered conflict-resolution training, and tried to tweak their job descriptions to minimize their interaction…all to no avail. It seemed to her that the harder she tried, the less motivated they were to find a solution for themselves.

When Cheryl finally brought the situation up in coaching, Bob told her about one of the iron laws of triangles that is most frequently broken by good leaders: **Efforts to will any other person(s) to change—or attempts to fix what is happening between the others in the triangle—almost always produce the opposite of what is intended and leave you with the stress that belongs to them**. The first triangle below illustrates the most common violation of this law.

Two direct reports are at odds, and the boss intervenes as the responsible party who tries to fix what is going on between them. The situation that Cheryl brought to Bob had reached such an impasse that she was losing sleep over it, spending time on weekends and evenings brooding over how to get the team members to cooperate, and so forth. It was the same situation Bridgette had been in when she learned from the work of Ed Friedman that this never works! The solution is illustrated by a second triangle.

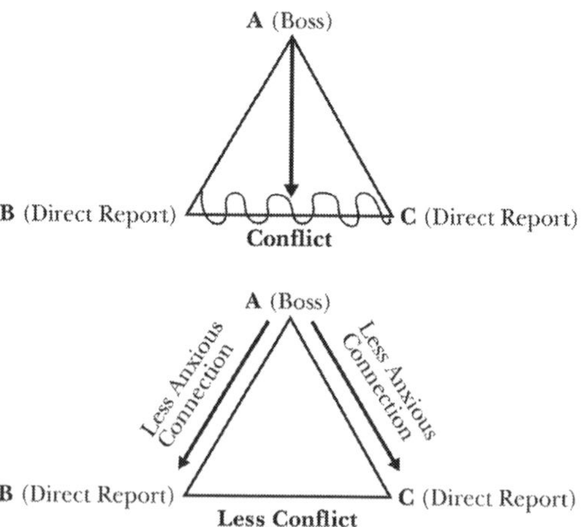

What Cheryl (and Bridgette) learned is that the best she could do was to reposition herself in the triangle by spelling out to each of the others very clearly and non-reactively what her expectations were and what they would be held accountable for, and then to step out of the role of fixer. Cheryl was successful when she communicated this to each of her reports individually and then again when all three were together. She spelled out what they were responsible for and indicated that whether they achieved their goals harmoniously or not was only of secondary interest to her. She said they could fix their impasse in any way they wished and that henceforth, she was not responsible for their feelings, only for holding them accountable for their job performance. (For more about Cheryl's approach, see Chapter 8 on Empathy.)

Bridgette found relief in much the same way, although not as a boss to direct reports. What she did was shift her mental model by frequent.ly reminding herself that she was not responsible for fixing the relationship between Doug and Sam. In fact, she needed to let them fix it themselves by letting go of overfunctioning on their behalf. She did not deliver any speeches about accountability to either of them; she simply tried to remain a neutral listener whenever one sought to get her to side with him. At most, she would gently suggest that they needed to talk directly to each other about their concerns, not to her. The relief she felt was almost immediate. And over a period of some months, she saw gradual but steady progress as they began to talk to each other more directly and work through issues as they arose rather than seek a toxic alliance with her.

STOP & REFLECT

- **Can you think of a healthy triangle you have been part of, either at home or at work? How did this triangle lower the anxiety of those involved, and to what extent did it promote clearer and calmer thinking?**
- **Can you think of a toxic triangle you have been part of—one that provoked escalating reactivity and made it more difficult for clear thinking to prevail? What role did you play in this triangle, and how did it impact your functioning?**

Third Big Idea—A New Way of LEADING: Manage your stress by repositioning yourself in triangles.

Bridgette was coaching Francis, the CEO of a start-up technology firm, and she also occasionally did leadership training for the three members of his senior leadership team: Sally, Marco, and Abdul. In the highly entrepreneurial culture of tech start-ups, everyone wore multiple hats: marketing and sales, product development, quality control, and so forth. The culture was fast-paced and competitive, and significant collaborative skills were required of every team member. Marco reached out to Bridgette for some coaching, and Francis was happy to approve and support his request.

Bridgette quickly discovered that Marco was on the verge of burnout. He told her that trying to keep up with the pace required of him was exhausting and that he was feeling more and more anxious about his relationships with Sally and Abdul, with whom he interacted closely on an almost daily basis. The problem, as he described it, was that both of them were more aggressive than he was, both in the area of marketing/sales and in the ambitious career goals that they pursued by "shamelessly" (Marco's word) currying favor with Francis. Marco loved the work and recognized his skills were more than adequate for the tasks he was responsible for, but he felt he was drowning and couldn't get a handle on why.

After a thorough intake session, Bridgette's assessment was that Marco needed to learn some basics about emotional triangles and especially how to reposition himself when a triangle starts to become toxic. She began by sharing with Marco her conviction that the cause of burnout is primarily emotional and not the result of the quantity of work an individual does. Upon questioning, Marco admitted that he was actually working fewer hours than in a previous job and that in that position, he had never felt overloaded and always showed up for work with high energy. His recognition that there was an emotional component to his burnout piqued his curiosity, and he was eager to learn about emotional triangles.

The cause of burnout is primarily emotional, and not the result of the quantity of work an individual does.

After explaining some of their basics, Bridgette described how anxiety moves around in triangles and that one's position in a triangle can make a dramatic difference in the amount of stress one absorbs. She quickly drew four triangles that represented situations Marco had described to her. As she did, she discussed with Marco the emotional dynamics in play within each situation.

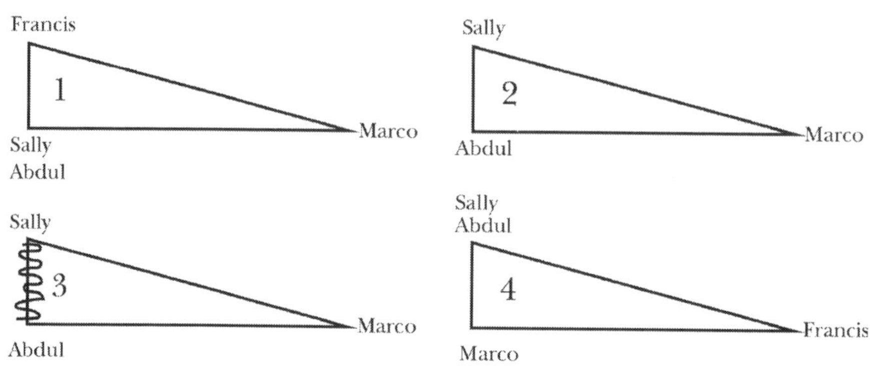

Triangle 1. Sally and Abdul are "currying favor" with Francis, and Marco is in the outsider position. It makes him feel terrible and left out, and he begins to question if he has the right stuff for his position.

Triangle 2. Sally and Abdul are interacting with each other, deploying their entrepreneurial strengths by going after some new business together, and they do not invite Marco into their brainstorming about how best to position an offer to the prospective client. Marco feels "worthless" (his words). Again, he is in the outsider position. It feels terrible and makes him anxious.

Triangle 3. Tensions are high because the visit to the prospective client went badly, and back at the office, in front of Marco, Sally and Abdul get into a heated argument and blame each other for dropping the ball. Marco is in the outsider position again, but this time he feels relieved and glad he was not involved.

Triangle 4. Sally and Abdul were given a new piece of work, and Francis is on their backs because they have not been able to get where he wants them after they already missed two deadlines. They discover it's an area of Marco's expertise from previous employment, and they ask for his help. Now Marco is in the insider position. He is at his best and can deliver the solution to them quickly. They thank him profusely for saving their butts, and he feels "great" (his word).

By the time Bridgette finished reviewing these examples, Marco understood how anxiety moves around in triangles and how important one's position is in each. Burnout, he understood, can come about from a variety of emotional dynamics:

- Feeling overly responsible for others or for what, in fact, is theirs—not yours—to worry about (as we discussed in the chapter on over- and underfunctioning)
- Being an outsider in a triangle where being an insider is perceived as essential for business success
- Being the one who is focused on in a way that channels the anxiety of the larger system in your direction
- Being the object of constant criticism or blame for problems not of your making (and beyond your ability or authority to fix)

Marco was also beginning to see that he had a say in what position he takes in a triangle—or at least a say in how he responds to the position he finds himself in. As the coaching session ended, he was already beginning to feel more hopeful. The prospect of being able to move out of the mood of burnout that had plagued him for months left him strongly motivated to learn more about triangles.

How to Reposition Yourself in Toxic Triangles

Bridgette brought to subsequent coaching sessions ideas to discuss with Marco about how to reposition himself in a triangle when he recognized it was more toxic than healthy. She cautioned him that knowing about how triangles work is not the same as developing the skills necessary to manage them, but it is a necessary first step. The key to developing the skills is to work at maintaining emotional neutrality, which is the best way to avoid getting hooked and stuck with the anxiety that a triangle is designed to spread around. These are some of the best practices that Bridgette shared with him that could help in his efforts to reposition himself within a toxic triangle:

- Work at developing relationships with each of the other two parts of the triangle when they are in conflict, but encourage them to resolve their own issues or differences rather than look to you for the solution.
- Try to understand both sides of the dynamic between the other two without taking sides.
- Avoid the "togetherness position" (Ed Friedman's phrase) where you feel responsible for keeping it all together.
- Be curious; try to draw out facts by asking good questions.
- Propose alternative ways to frame/see/understand the situation.
- Work at clarifying someone's position rather than changing others' minds or agreeing/disagreeing with others.
- Don't get attached to any particular outcome.
- Don't disconnect or rescue; remain available as a resource while encouraging others to reach a resolution.
- Avoid feeling sorry for, blaming, or thinking about what "should be."

It is important to keep in mind that when we urge leaders to maintain emotional neutrality in the triangles they are part of, we are not suggesting that they abdicate their responsibility for providing clarity on key issues. A leader may need to make an unpopular decision or take a clear stand on a policy or approach in order to resolve the conflict that is embedded within a triangle. However, this should be done in such a way that is not about taking sides with one or another of the persons involved. This requires keen self-awareness and great sensitivity on the part of the leader as well as skillful communication to all parties.

Our experience has shown us time and again that when a leader makes a clear call, even those who disagree with the decision eventually calm down and align themselves with the direction the leader is taking, provided they have had an opportunity to voice their perspectives and know that they have been genuinely heard.

STOP & REFLECT

- **Take a look at the best practices we've listed above to reposition yourself in a toxic triangle. Which one or two of these practices do you most want to incorporate into the way you manage yourself in triangles?**
- **How might doing so lower your stress and improve your effectiveness?**
- **Where do you have an opportunity to reposition yourself in a stressful triangle by being the "third person" described in this quote from Murray Bowen? "Conflict between two people will resolve automatically if both remain in emotional contact with a third person who can relate actively to both without taking sides."**

Core Practices

Hit the Pause Button before Triangulating

Next time you are about to involve a third party in an anxious situation, pause to reflect on the impact your actions will have on yourself, the other person, and the system at large.

Practice Emotional Neutrality

Next time someone involves you in a triangle, resist the temptation to take his/her side. Instead, listen openly, offer suggestions (if appropriate) for how s/he might address the issue directly with the other person, and express confidence in her/his ability to handle the situation. Maintaining emotional neutrality lowers the anxiety in the triangle and helps everyone to think more clearly about the best path forward.

Chapter Summary

- Triangles are the foundation of every relationship system, and they are everywhere! Rather than try to avoid them altogether, resilient leaders work instead to reposition themselves in triangles in a way that lowers anxiety and promotes healthier functioning for all.
- How well leaders manage themselves in triangles is the key to lowering their stress and improving their health and effectiveness.
- Because the emotional systems of families and organizations operate according to the same principles, the strategies for managing oneself in triangles is the same in both places.
- Every triangle is formed out of a desire to alleviate the anxiety that is being experienced by two people (or two groups) by spreading it out over a larger geography.
- A key to healthy functioning in triangles is to avoid feeling responsible for fixing or solving what is happening between those on the other side of the triangle.
- Triangles can be healthy or toxic. A triangle is toxic to the extent that it escalates, rather than lowers, the anxiety that originally gave rise to it. In addition to raising stress levels, a toxic triangle keeps those involved stuck in old patterns of thinking, relating, and behaving.
- A key tenet of managing triangles is to develop the skill of maintaining emotional neutrality. A resilient leader resists taking sides in a triangle but *does* take a clear stand on an issue that needs resolving. The former is about one's position in the emotional system, while the latter is about bringing clarity to the rational system.
- If you (or someone you manage) are experiencing unusually high levels of stress and anxiety, chances are good you are stuck in a toxic triangle. The first step to changing this is to get curious about the triangle you are in, observe the position you are playing in it, and reposition yourself using one or more of the strategies we've shared in this chapter.

CHAPTER 7

GENERATION TO GENERATION
YESTERDAY'S GHOSTS, TODAY'S REALITY, TOMORROW'S OPPORTUNITIES

Our lives are so important to us that we tend to think the story of them begins with our birth. First, there was nothing, then I was born... Yet that is not so. Human lives are not pieces of string that can be separated out from a knot of others and laid out straight. Families are webs. Impossible to touch one part of it without setting the rest vibrating. Impossible to understand one part without having a sense of the whole.

—Diane Setterfield
The Thirteenth Tale

Throughout this book, we have defined Resilient Leadership as a New Way of SEEING, THINKING, and LEADING that helps leaders navigate the hidden dynamics of organizations more effectively.

As we begin this chapter, we want to return briefly to the second part of our definition, which speaks to what resilient leaders can *do*. As they grow and become increasingly self-differentiated, resilient leaders are able to:

- lead with calm, clarity, and conviction in the midst of anxiety provoked by increasing complexity and accelerating change.
- lead from strength. They know how to care for themselves emotionally, spiritually, and physically and sustain their leadership efforts over time.

In Chapter 2, we explored how a leader can act as a step-down transformer of the chronic anxiety in his/her organization, bringing a greater sense of *calm* and *thoughtfulness* to anxious situations. In chapters 3 and 4, we talked about leading with *clarity and conviction* while still staying connected to the important people and stakeholders the leader wishes to influence. But what does the definition mean when it says to "lead from strength," and how might this chapter you are about to read shed light on this?

Strengths and Vulnerabilities

Each of us has strengths that we bring to bear in our roles as leaders. In this chapter, we'll explore the notion of our *inherited* strengths—those that originate from the people and relationship systems that came before us (our parents, grandparents, and extended family members) whose patterns of relating to one another shaped us in profound and often positive ways.

We'll also look at the vulnerabilities that we may have inherited from the past—those default tendencies that we bring with us to any emotional system and that can so easily get triggered without our full awareness or explicit consent!

When we step back and identify both our inherited strengths and our inherited vulnerabilities, we can see more clearly how they impact our current functioning both at work and at home. When that happens, we become more resilient, more flexible, and more at choice in the important leadership stands we take. This is what it means to lead from strength.

First Big Idea—A New Way of SEEING: Recognize the extent to which your leadership reflects your inherited strengths and vulnerabilities from previous generations.

Bob was coaching Kevin and helping him and his team with a very important strategic planning initiative. At a certain point, Kevin asked Bob if he would also coach Dave, one of his high-potential leaders who had recently begun to falter. "I don't know what's going on with Dave, but in the last few months, the quality of his work has fallen off dramatically, and I'm getting all sorts of complaints from other team members about his negative attitude."

When Bob asked Dave if he'd be interested in some coaching, he was quick to accept the invitation. "I'd love it," he said. "I am really asking myself if I belong on this team, and maybe you can help me sort some things out." By the end of their third coaching session, here's what had come to light: Dave was very angry with Kevin for the way he had "abandoned [him]" (Dave's words). Kevin had been telling Dave that he was a prime candidate for advancement and informally mentoring him for the better part of a year until several months ago. "Then all of a sudden, he's too busy to see me—offered some lame excuse about being busy, and out of the blue has just cut me off." And, when asked if he had talked about this with Kevin, Dave just shrugged and said, "Why bother? I've seen his kind before. If I'm going to make it in this company, I've got to do it on my own."

The intensity of Dave's feelings puzzled Bob, and he shared his observation with Dave that his anger seemed disproportionate, given the circumstances that Dave had described. Bob inquired if there was something more going on that he was missing. The story that Dave then shared made it immediately clear what was behind his reactivity: "When my father was fifteen years old, he came home from school one day and discovered that my grandmother had abandoned the family. My grandfather was blindsided, and in the months and years that followed, Dad was left with more than his fair share of responsibility for raising his two younger sisters. My grandfather drilled it into Dad's head that if he was going to survive in life, he should never count on another person—only himself. That's a lesson Dad taught all of us growing up as well: when it comes down to it, you should never depend on anyone else, and don't be surprised when someone lets you down, even someone you thought you could count on."

What's Going On Here?

Over the course of several more coaching sessions, Bob was able to help Dave reflect a bit more thoughtfully on the circumstances of his "abandonment" by Kevin and his reaction to it. Dave was able to recognize that it was much more than Kevin's behavior that triggered him and that the intensity of his reactivity was not in his own best interest. Bob shared with Dave a new perspective on how to think about some of the strengths and vulnerabilities he brought to his professional life and their roots in his family inheritance stretching back to his grandfather's failed marriage.

Who we are as adults and as leaders is the result of many factors. The old debate about whether nature or nurture contributes more to our makeup will continue to occupy researchers, but what we can say for certain is that both have an indispensable role to play in the process of our growth and development. Science is discovering daily how much our genes determine everything from our physical appearance to how our body functions across our lifespan. Our environment also shapes us in decisive ways, from the family and culture into which we are born and raised to the random life experiences that can strengthen or traumatize us.

Bob suggested to Dave that he might profit from reflecting on how the emotional system he had inherited from previous generations of his family also bequeathed to him important strengths and vulnerabilities—from his level of self-differentiation to the unconscious triggers behind his automatic, reactive behaviors. Dave admired his grandfather's resilience after being deserted by his wife. The "old man" had gone on to raise his three children with strong values, and all had very successful personal and professional lives. Dave also recognized how much he was like his father and grandfather in his self-reliance, his can-do attitude, and his strong work ethic. His professional achievements were testimony to those qualities, and he admitted to Bob that Kevin had highlighted exactly those characteristics when he had spoken to him about his leadership potential and offered to mentor him.

Dave recognized how much he was like his father and grandfather in his self-reliance, his "can-do" attitude, and his strong work ethic.

Bob and Dave also discussed some of the vulnerabilities passed on to him as part of his multigenerational family system. The shadow side of his self-reliance came from the anxiety of his grandfather and his father around the possibility of betrayal and abandonment. Rather than talking over with Kevin the reasons that he'd needed to pull back from their mentoring, Dave had reacted with an intensity that spilled over into his job performance and even into relationships with colleagues on his team—all to his detriment. The distress that made him say to Bob, "I am really asking myself if I belong on this team," was a disproportionate, reactive stance more than an objective assessment of the opportunities and liabilities in his current situation. They also discussed how the strength of his self-reliance carried a hidden tendency to overfunction in ways that were more anxiety-driven than thoughtful and proactive.

Developing a greater self-awareness of the strengths and vulnerabilities that we inherit from the emotional systems of previous generations of our family does not require getting into therapy or a degree in psychology. What it does require is our attention and our conviction that the insights we can derive from this kind of awareness will serve us well in all of the key relationship systems to which we belong. Just as the many professional assessments that identify key competencies for career success can help us make better job choices, so too a deeper knowledge of the strengths and vulnerabilities we inherit from the emotional systems of previous generations of our family can enrich our ability to leverage those strengths and better manage our vulnerabilities—both at home and at work.

STOP & REFLECT

- **Think about the strengths you possess as a leader—those qualities and attributes that help you to lead and inspire others when you are at your best. To what extent might one or more of those strengths be part of your inheritance from the emotional systems of previous generations of your family?**
- **What are some of your vulnerabilities as a leader—the characteristics you default to when you are triggered by challenging people or circumstances and you are at**

your worst? To what extent might one or more of these vulnerabilities be part of your inheritance from the emotional systems of previous generations?

- **How might reflecting on your inherited strengths and vulnerabilities help you lead more thoughtfully?**

Second Big Idea—A New Way of THINKING: Understand the inherited strengths and vulnerabilities of the systems you lead.

Just as we inherit strengths and vulnerabilities from the emotional systems of previous generations of our family, the organizational systems we lead also reflect the presence of the past—in ways that can work both for us and against us. Resilient leaders who can view their organizations through this "past lens" learn to recognize the inherited strengths in their systems that they can draw upon as well as the potential pitfalls from vulnerabilities passed down by previous generations.

Bridgette was brought in to help Monica, the new owner and CEO of a once very successful mechanical engineering firm that was struggling to recover from a near-catastrophic power struggle between its two founding partners, Jim and Tony. Over fifteen years, the two partners had built a highly creative and entrepreneurial organization that attracted top talent and steadily built an impressive portfolio of high-end clients. The partners had quite different personalities: Jim was steady, low-key, fiscally conservative, and had an eye for detail. Tony was outgoing and volatile, a creative

> **Just as we inherit strengths and vulnerabilities from the emotional systems of previous generations of our family, the organizational systems we lead also reflect the presence of the past, in ways that can work both for us and against us.**

thinker, and a risk-taker. But they managed to complement one another as each brought his best and contributed equally to the success of the business.

About five years earlier, the relationship between Jim and Tony had blown up over financial management issues where they held widely divergent viewpoints. Their friendship soured as they butted heads over many months, and in the end, the only solution they came up with was for Jim to buy out Tony's share of the company. Tony left Jim with a heavily leveraged business and a sizeable contingent of employees who were angry at how Jim had treated him. A number of those unhappy employees left the organization shortly thereafter to work with Tony in a new venture. But even among those who remained, communications and teamwork remained at an all-time low.

Almost a year before she engaged Bridgette, Monica had purchased the company from Jim. At their first meeting, she confided to Bridgette, "I feel like I work in a battle zone. For God's sake, it's been five years since the blowup, and new hires invariably get pulled into one or the other of the remaining groups of old-timers who are still keeping the founders' feud alive. The talent and the potential of this organization is phenomenal, but if we don't learn how to work together again, our future as an organization is pretty bleak."

What's Going On Here?

In the First Big Idea, we described how Dave came to an understanding of the powerful influence that previous generations of his family had on his reactivity at work. Monica's story will allow us to see how that same process of inherited patterns occurs in organizational families. Our work with senior leaders over many years has convinced us that this is often one of the most challenging tasks for a leader who seeks to practice a new way of SEEING and THINKING.

Organizations are not families, even though they share many of the same characteristics and operate according to many of the same immutable principles of how emotional systems function. Members of families always remain connected by ties of blood and marriage, even across hundreds of years. But when someone leaves an organization, even after a long tenure, the connections are rarely maintained for very long. What does remain, however, are the emotional patterns that have been embedded especially by senior leaders, particularly by founders who shaped the company's early functioning. For subsequent generations of leaders who join it years later, becoming aware of the continuing presence and power of those patterns—and their origins in previous generations—may seem to be a daunting and even impossible task.

Understanding the Presence of the Past

The emotional system of a workplace, like that in a family system, exerts a powerful, hidden influence on those who join the "family" at any point in the organization's history. Smart onboarding programs often do a good job of introducing new hires to more than company policies and procedures. They cover stories of the founders and other turning points (mergers, technological breakthroughs, responses to heroic challenges, and so on) in the history of the organization and in general seek to share the culture of the organization in ways that make for a smoother transition and more rapid assimilation of new employees. But we have yet to encounter an organization that recognizes, let alone knows how to share with newcomers, the most powerful forces that have shaped the way the organization functions in the present—the inherited patterns of its emotional system.

What we have seen, however, is what happens when we coach a senior leader who has understood the power of this phenomenon in family life and who then sets out to understand more deeply how the same phenomenon is at work in the organization s/he leads. It takes a different level of questions and a different kind of research to recognize inherited strengths and vulnerabilities in the workplace. But it can be done. The following story illustrates how a senior leader's focus on the emotional system of the workplace can reap rich rewards.

Bob, Bridgette, and others from their RL team worked on a multiyear deployment of Resilient Leadership training and coaching in a large federal agency undergoing a very significant reorganization involving the realignment of core programs, job responsibilities, reporting structures, and so forth. One of the senior leaders, Kwan, was a strong supporter of the Resilient Leadership model and recognized that the work being done to improve the agency's rational system could easily fail to achieve its goal unless long-standing patterns in the emotional system were also addressed.

Kwan had been wanting to bring this point home to others on his senior leadership team when he ran across a report done by outside consultants more than thirty years earlier as part of an efficiency study of his office. He was struck by the similarities in the issues described in the report and the challenges that the current leadership team had been discussing as part of the reorganization. He removed the cover page of the report and had it copied and distributed to members of the team for discussion at their next meeting. He opened the meeting by asking if the team members thought the report was an accurate description of the challenges that had to be dealt with for the reorganization to be successful. Without exception, all agreed that the report was accurate in naming the current issues they needed to address!

Kwan was smart enough not to prolong the mild deception he had used to drive home his point with his colleagues that working on the rational system alone would not solve all of the long-standing operational issues that previous generations had tried to resolve. He reminded the group of the RL training they had received and the iceberg diagram that spoke to how massive is the impact of the emotional system on any attempts to implement changes in the rational system. Beneath the issues that were still in place thirty years later were patterns of strengths and vulnerabilities from the emotional system that none of the previous generations of leaders had addressed directly. The conversation opened up a whole new level of inquiry and brought forth from the leadership team fresh insights about how to facilitate the implementation of the planned reorganization. It would not be possible to measure the impact of that new awareness on the part of the senior leaders, especially given the complexity and size of all the moving parts involved in that large-scale change initiative. But from Kwan's perspective, the result was positive and brought a new awareness of organizational strengths and vulnerabilities to the work being done by key decision-makers in the organization.

The Rest of Monica's Story

We return now to the story of Monica and how that same shift of awareness helped her as a new leader to deal with inherited patterns in her company. Bridgette coached Monica and worked with her leadership team over the next two years. She introduced them to the key Resilient Leadership idea that organizations are made up of both rational and emotional systems, and she did both coaching and training around the effects of high levels of chronic anxiety and reactivity, the importance of showing up as a less anxious presence and acting as a step-down transformer, the toxic potential of interlocking (anxious) triangles, and self-management practices that promote a calmer, more thoughtful presence. Most importantly, she helped them to think systems and to understand how organizations, like families, carry within their emotional systems both strengths and vulnerabilities from previous generations.

Most important, she helped them to think systems.

A few of the more well-differentiated members of the leadership team began to get it and grew steadily in their ability to take strong stands whenever behaviors symptomatic of the lingering residue from Jim and Tony surfaced. They held one another accountable for what Monica insisted was going to be the "new normal" of civility, collaboration, communication, and creative engagement ("Monica's 4 C's").

In one memorable weekend-planning retreat that they later referred to as a "watershed," Bridgette led the leadership team through an exercise in which they named the strengths of the organization that remained as part of Jim and Tony's legacy as well as the vulnerabilities that still haunted their efforts at becoming a high-performance organization. Bridgette discussed with them the potential benefits of adopting a research focus on the history of how the organization had functioned over time. She urged each person before coming to the retreat to talk to three others who had been in the organization for at least ten years as a way of gathering a more objective picture of the organization as it had been in both good times and in times of crisis. She suggested that they ask questions such as these:

- How much anxiety was present in the system at different times, and how did it manifest itself?
- Were there events or situations that increased anxiety or that helped to lower it? What was the role of leaders in either situation?
- What kind of reactive behaviors most often characterize this organization during tough times?
- What are the resources within the organization that have helped it to recover better or faster from a crisis?
- Who have been the informal leaders who have most influenced the company during its best times? How did they do that?
- What stories best embody the finest hours of the organization?

When Bridgette first brought up the idea of incorporating this exercise into the retreat, she got a good bit of pushback. Some were leery of opening what they called "a can of worms." Various other reasons were put forth for why it was not the best use of time, didn't seem relevant, and so forth. She persisted and even wondered aloud if she was hearing some anxiety that was more about the ghosts of the past than about what would be of most value for the team retreat. She made her case for such an exercise by pointing out the potential benefits:

- Getting on the balcony as an observer can establish a more objective perspective.
- A curious stance can lower reactivity and help a system get unstuck from a prior event that continues to ripple down through generations.
- The process of gathering information can contribute to more thoughtfulness in the system as questions are asked that transcend reactive frameworks of the past.
- The thoughtfulness required of a research perspective is inherently a calming force.
- Doing this kind of research can support an individual's (or a team's) efforts at offering more well-differentiated leadership for the system at large.

Thinking Systems

What most impressed Bridgette, in the end, was that both lists that the team eventually came up with at the retreat contained as many themes related to the emotional system as to the rational system. They had the courage to get on the balcony to spot yesterday's ghosts, and they even discovered more inherited strengths than vulnerabilities. This awareness reinforced in the team a spirit of optimism about the company's opportunities going forward.

Monica's leadership was key to her team's ability to "think systems" as they observed and then understood at a deeper level the presence and power of certain inherited patterns that were embedded in the emotional system of the organization. She helped them to focus on and name the legacy—both strengths and vulnerabilities—of Jim and Tony and to understand the extent to which those inherited patterns continued to influence even new hires who came on board long after the founders had departed. Gradually, but very steadily, the team experienced firsthand the power of a sustained, intentional effort to rediscover resources within the system of the organization that would allow them to embrace new behaviors and move beyond a "stuck" focus on the reactive patterns of the past.

Leaders like Monica who can understand the strengths and vulnerabilities of the system they are responsible for are in a much stronger position to influence that system for the better—to build on inherited strengths and to reduce the influence of inherited vulnerabilities. We describe the emotional system as the hidden chemistry of an organization because it operates nearly always beneath our conscious awareness. But when, at the conscious awareness level, a leader learns to observe default patterns of reactivity that signal increased anxiety—and also understands the power of those patterns to influence current behavior—then that hidden chemistry is laid bare. With this information and perspective in hand, a well-differentiated leader can promote significant, lasting change in the emotional system.

Leaders who are able to understand the strengths and vulnerabilities of the system they are responsible for are in a much stronger position to influence that system for the better.

Identifying Organizational Strengths and Vulnerabilities

An astute leader can learn to recognize and understand the kinds of patterns that are indicative of the strengths and vulnerabilities embedded in the emotional system of an organization. These patterns can be subtle or blatant. They can support the healthy flourishing of the organization or remain unseen pitfalls ever ready to subvert the system's success. Among the organizational **strengths** that a skilled leader might recognize are:

- Capacity for risk-taking
- Stamina to persist in pursuit of important goals or values
- Ability to withstand criticism and ridicule in the short term for long-term benefits
- Playfulness and use of humor to calm down
- Decisiveness
- Adventurousness
- Innovative spirit that encourages creativity

And here are some of the organizational **vulnerabilities** that a leader might recognize:

- Over/underfunctioning
- Distancing and cutoffs
- Fusing and groupthink
- Anxious triangles
- Comforting, rescuing, or tolerating underperformers
- Silos, "us versus them" mentality
- Too much or too little conflict
- Quickness to blame others
- Failure to take responsibility for self
- Preference for the quick fix

Which of these patterns is part of the hidden legacy of your organization? How might you as a leader leverage those that are strengths? And how might you neutralize—or at least minimize—the influence of those that are vulnerabilities?

When last we checked back with Monica, she reported a steady three-year climb in the company's profitability. With her characteristic sense of humor, she said that the "war zone" she had inherited was "not yet the Garden of Eden, but it sure feels like peace and prosperity are in our future!"

STOP & REFLECT

- **Think about a time when your organization was at its best. What positive qualities or behaviors did you see emerge in the system, and how did these strengths make a difference for you and others? Which of these strengths do you think were inherited from previous generations of leaders and their way of interacting with others in the system?**
- **Think about a time when your organization was at its worst. What patterns of reactivity emerged that hindered you and others from taking thoughtful action? To what extent do you see these patterns of reactivity still at work today?**

Third Big Idea—A New Way of LEADING: Strengthen the systems you lead by leveraging your inherited strengths and mitigating your inherited vulnerabilities.

Acting as a resilient leader is as much an art as it is a science, and if we get it right only 50 percent of the time…well, how many pros do you know who bat .500 regularly? This Third Big Idea suggests that it is not enough for leaders to recognize and understand the influence of previous generations on the emotional systems of which they are a part; they must also deploy that knowledge by leading in new and more effective ways. This is tricky business, because leaders show up at work carrying strengths and vulnerabilities from their own multigenerational family systems, and then they are expected to act in ways that promote healthier functioning in an organizational system with its own inherited strengths and vulnerabilities. The complexity of this balancing act is obvious, but when Resilient Leadership is practiced daily both at home and at work over a sustained period, the likelihood of getting it right more often than not is high.

Acting as a resilient leader is as much an art as it is a science.

Bob worked for almost ten years in an organization that embraced Resilient Leadership as one of its core leadership competencies. Virtually all of the top leaders in the organization received extended coaching during those years, and hundreds more underwent RL training and worked at practicing it on a regular basis.

One of the leaders Bob coached, Lynette, took a strong interest in the way that the principles of Resilient Leadership could be practiced at home as well as at work. She had done a good bit of research into her own family systems and had come to recognize in herself a pattern of very strong women who consistently functioned as rescuers for family members as well as for many others in the tight-knit local community where the family had lived for more than a century. She saw this as one of the strengths she brought to her leadership role at work as well, and she could cite numerous instances in which she was able to step forward and take charge of a situation when others were hesitant or ill-equipped to do so.

The organization had as one of its core values the well-being and support of every employee, and for Lynette, this often meant working to help underperforming members of her staff "above and beyond" (her words) what most managers would be willing to do. The corporate culture gave a green light for this tendency in Lynette, but the truth was that the company's admirable concern for employees had a shadow side: leaders frequently tolerated poor performance and failed to hold employees accountable for behaviors that should have been stopped with direct feedback or even dealt with through termination.

Off and on over nearly a year, Bob and Lynette had been discussing one of her direct reports whose performance was below acceptable standards. Lynette, time and again, gave the employee "one more chance" by offering extra training, the personalized support of a special mentor, and other rescuing efforts. When virtually all of the employee's peers finally demanded Lynette take action, she reluctantly terminated the employee.

What's Going On Here?

In a subsequent coaching session where Bob and Lynette reflected on her prolonged but futile efforts to rescue the employee, Lynette was finally able to recognize how deep the connection was between an inherited "strength" from her family system (as a strong and caring woman) and her workplace pattern of anxiety-driven overfunctioning on behalf of a classic underfunctioner. She also recognized the vulnerability embedded in the organization's core value of caring for employees and how that had made it easier for her to justify the shadow side of the "strength" she had inherited from her family system. Lynette realized that anxiety-based conflict avoidance and overfunctioning played a part in both home and work systems and that the convergence of the two systems' vulnerabilities had contributed to "the mess [she had] made of it" (her words).

Life is messy, and it took some genuine soul-searching on Lynette's part to sort things out and recognize how an unconscious inherited pattern can be both a strength and a vulnerability. When she was finally able to get in touch with the role that anxiety was playing in both of her emotional systems, her appreciation grew significantly for the automatic nature of these deep-seated patterns. She was determined, however, to become more intentional about leveraging her strength and minimizing her vulnerability. She put in place several steps to avoid the trap of a seductive strength that hid a dangerous vulnerability:

- She determined to use her regular meetings with direct reports more proactively and self-monitor her tendency to put off necessary feedback when their performance was not up to par.
- She recommitted to several calming practices that she knew always helped lower her overall anxiety levels (but that had fallen off of her busy daily routine).
- She discussed with her supervisor the insight she had come to and asked him to hold her accountable when he observed her slipping back into overfunctioning or conflict-avoidance patterns.
- She started to talk more openly with senior-level colleagues about the shadow side of the company's core value regarding employees and how it was an unspoken vulnerability with hidden costs they should not tolerate.
- She volunteered with Bob to do an "RL case study" of her experience during a senior-team in-service meeting.

STOP & REFLECT

- **What were some of the unspoken maxims in your family growing up (e.g., "Keep the peace at all costs.")?**
- **How might those unwritten family rules be influencing the way you lead now, for better or worse?**

Core Practices

Observe Your Inherited Vulnerabilities
Whenever you find yourself with an intensity that is disproportionate to a triggering event, pause to reflect:

- What provoked me?
- Is my reactivity connected to a vulnerability I've inherited from the past? If so, what is the vulnerability?
- What is the impact on me, others, and my system?
- How might I mitigate this vulnerability going forward?

Observe Your Inherited Strengths
Whenever you overcome a significant challenge or succeed in taking advantage of a significant opportunity, pause to consider:

- What strengths was I able to bring to bear in the situation?
- Are any of these strengths ones I have inherited from previous generations in my family system?
- How might I be even more intentional about leveraging them in my role as a leader?

Chapter Summary

- Resilient leaders recognize the extent to which their leadership, for better and for worse, reflects the presence (and the influence) of the past—those patterned tendencies that have been handed down from both their family system and their work system.
- Inherited strengths are those attributes and capabilities that we possess when we are at our best—and that originate from the people and relationship systems that came before us.
- Inherited vulnerabilities are those default tendencies we possess when we are at our worst—and that originate from the people and relationship systems that came before us. Such tendencies are easily triggered without our awareness or explicit consent.
- Resilient leaders mindfully work to leverage their inherited strengths and to mitigate their inherited vulnerabilities. Doing so enables them to lead from strength and to sustain their leadership efforts over time.
- Organizations, just like leaders and families, carry within their emotional systems both strengths and vulnerabilities from previous generations.
- Leaders who are able to understand the strengths and vulnerabilities of the system they are responsible for are in a much stronger position to influence that system for the better. They do this by working (often with others) to build on inherited strengths and to reduce the influence of inherited vulnerabilities.

CHAPTER 8

AVOID THE EMPATHY TRAP
KNOW WHEN EMPATHY WORKS AND WHEN IT WILL BACKFIRE

More hurtfulness to others is done in the service of pious helpfulness than in the name of malevolent intent.

—Murray Bowen
Family Therapy in Clinical Practice

Ed Friedman was developing many of his ideas on leadership (published posthumously in *A Failure of Nerve*) during the years that Bob was part of one of Ed's ongoing leadership-development seminars. Bob recalls the passion with which Ed spoke about what he called the "fallacy of empathy" and how he framed his ideas on empathy as part of a much, much larger issue than the ability of any particular leader to abstain from being overly empathic. In the chapter of his book that deals with this issue, he asserts that what is at stake on the most fundamental level is "the struggle between good and evil, between life and death, between what is destructive and what is creative, between dependency and responsibility…between what is evolutionary and what is regressive" (page 143 of the 2017 revised edition). This provocative assertion raised many an eyebrow, but Ed chose his words carefully, and he believed strongly that well-differentiated leaders would be the key to moving us forward and out of the escalating chaos overtaking every major institution of our society—indeed, of our world.

Ed called for a fundamental reorientation of leaders away from several of the major "fallacies" that he described in the book. Those fallacies, he believed, undermine the kind of leadership necessary to reverse the regressive forces that threaten institutions of every scale: from families coping with the destruction inflicted from within by their most poorly differentiated members; to organizations large and small whose vitality and creativity is sapped by efforts required to deal with their chronic troublemakers; to society on a global scale, destabilized and thrown into chaos by threats from the likes of organized crime, terrorists, and totalitarian states armed with weapons of mass destruction.

> ***The Fallacy of Empathy:***
> **The mistaken belief that offering support, understanding, and comfort (to poorly differentiated others) will, by itself, promote in them greater responsibility for self.**

We share Ed's conviction that our world is facing terrible threats in these days. Likewise, we have seen firsthand the tremendous difference that well-differentiated leaders can make in organizations of every size and sort. Whatever misguided understandings of leadership persist today need to be challenged and done away with. We rank the fallacy of empathy high among those misguided notions that can hobble and even destroy the best efforts of well-intentioned leaders.

We define the *fallacy of empathy* as "the mistaken belief that offering support, understanding, and comfort (especially to the poorly differentiated) will, by itself, promote in them greater responsibility for self." Promoting greater responsibility in others for self (and for results) is an essential part of being a resilient leader. Those who fall prey to the fallacy of empathy struggle to promote responsibility for self in others and ultimately produce the opposite effect.

Our warnings about misguided, ill-timed, or excessive empathy should in no way be interpreted as an indictment of a leader's appropriate expressions of empathy.

However, it is important to state at the outset our equally firm conviction that compassion for others and a capacity for authentic caring are also essential for leadership effectiveness. What we say below by way of warning about misguided, ill-timed, or excessive empathy on the part of a leader should in no way be interpreted as an indictment of a leader's appropriate expressions of empathy or initiatives to take specific actions that embody a caring response to someone genuinely in need of support.

First Big Idea—A New Way of SEEING: Observe whether your default tendency is to offer comfort or challenge.

Bob was called in by the board chair of a failing nonprofit to see if he could support the CEO, Roger, who was becoming desperate in his search for a solution to the looming insolvency. Bob worked with Roger for about six months until it became clear that Roger was neither motivated nor capable of making the kind of changes necessary to turn the situation around. Less than a year later, the organization had collapsed and the entire workforce was scrambling to find employment. Here's what happened:

Thirty years earlier, Roger had founded the organization based on an innovative approach to providing resources for at-risk young people in a poor section of a large urban center. Through a combination of Roger's inspired leadership, numerous government contracts, and some very generous foundation grants, the organization grew rapidly and earned a well-deserved reputation for the good work it was accomplishing. Roger attracted many mission-driven workers, and despite his limited ability to manage certain aspects of the growing pains typical of a start-up, the first ten years of the organization were very successful.

As Roger told Bob when describing his management philosophy, "We're like family here. We are all committed to the mission, and I've never had to fire anyone." What Bob discovered, however, was that Roger was very conflict-avoidant and in years past had failed to terminate several egregious cases of malfeasance on the part of two veteran employees who were still in leadership positions. Nor had he held accountable those on his team who were chronic underperformers. When Bob asked about this, Roger's mantra was, "We're family, and you don't just get rid of family when they make a mistake."

Bob also learned from several team members that morale was very low among those most dedicated to the organization's success. They worked hard and saw how many of their colleagues were just along for the ride and rarely put in a full day's work, knowing they would never get fired. When pressed to take action and make the necessary staff changes, Roger's consistent response had been to try (repeatedly) to motivate the problem employees with kindness and even undeserved cash incentives. Roger was the poster child for failed leadership due to the fallacy of empathy, and both his employees and the at-risk young people who looked to his organization for help were ultimately the ones who paid the consequences of his shortcomings.

Roger's story is perhaps an extreme example of someone whose leadership repertoire was so narrowly limited that he found it virtually impossible to hold his employees accountable or even to offer mild challenges when they were off track. The reasons that his capacity was so limited in this regard no doubt came from a combination of factors—his innate personality, family patterns absorbed early on, later life experiences, values espoused as he grew into adulthood, and so forth. The fact is, each of us has a given capacity and innate tendency that inclines us toward challenge or comfort, accountability or empathy. Like other key leadership competencies, this is an area that deserves our attention. The more self-aware we are of what we are unconsciously inclined to prefer, the better able we are to be at choice as to whether we follow those spontaneous tendencies or thoughtfully consider other alternatives.

Each of us has a given capacity and an innate tendency that inclines us toward challenge or comfort, accountability or empathy.

Consider the following responses that a leader might make when faced with a difficult employee or a complex situation that requires the leader to take a stand:

Actions That Comfort

- Express empathy and compassion for the person's struggle
- Listen non-judgmentally
- Offer support/resources
- Step in to assist
- Share her/his own experience with struggle or pain
- Take the person's side if the challenge is with others
- Express his/her belief in the person
- Intervene on behalf of the person with others who are challenging her/him

Actions That Challenge

- Allow natural consequences to prevail, even when painful
- Ask what the person really wants and if s/he is willing to work for a better outcome
- Establish clear expectations and hold the person accountable
- Create opportunities that require people to think/act outside of their comfort zone
- Provide timely, constructive feedback that enables someone to course-correct
- Express her/his dissatisfaction with the status quo and communicate a better future

Which of these do you think you typically find easier to do? Of course, the specific circumstances of every situation are highly relevant when we are deciding whether to offer comfort or challenge and so the ideal is that a leader has a broad repertoire of options with which s/he is comfortable when a response is required. But what is your default tendency? And how easily do you move in that direction without ever considering that perhaps a different kind of response is really what is most needed and appropriate, given all that you know about the person and the situation? Our First Big Idea suggests that if you can observe and be mindful of your default tendency, you are more likely to be free to choose a more thoughtful and appropriate response rather than an automatic, reactive one. Furthermore, the best practice in most situations usually involves a healthy balance of both challenge and comfort, with one or the other getting a bit more emphasis depending on individual circumstances.

STOP & REFLECT

- **Can you think of a time when you were part of a situation in which the leader's efforts to be empathetic and compassionate resulted in a person becoming more helpless and dependent rather than more responsible?**
- **What is your default tendency—to offer comfort or to offer challenge?**

Second Big Idea—A New Way of THINKING: Understand that leaders must set boundaries for the poorly differentiated.

Bridgette once worked with a client, Erik, whose family of origin had been deeply impacted by his sister's failure to grow into a responsible adult. He shared with Bridgette the story of his sister because he was concerned about the way that certain family patterns were influencing his behavior at work. His sister was the only girl, with three male siblings, and from early on, her parents indulged her and failed to hold her accountable for her poor behavior and lapses in judgment. Without realizing it, her loving parents had been setting her up for a lifetime of struggle as an adult due to the way that they constantly shielded her from any significant challenges.

When she became pregnant in high school, her parents stepped in and dealt with every aspect of her pregnancy and the subsequent adoption. The more they "helped" her by protecting her from the consequences of many immature behaviors as a growing young adult, the more she struggled socially, academically, and financially. Eventually, she became involved in alcohol and drugs, was unable to hold a steady job, and continued to rely on her parents for support in nearly every dimension of her life. No matter how many resources they provided to her, she never demonstrated a willingness to take responsibility for her life circumstances. Nor did her parents set appropriate boundaries for her. As a result, well into adulthood, she remained a disruptive force for the entire family system. Even as a grown adult in her forties, she was still receiving financial aid from them. By now, her siblings had grown resentful of her, and her parents were showing the strain of her relentless neediness.

Understanding the Poorly Differentiated

Erik brought this family story to his coaching with Bridgette because he recognized that his reactivity was often triggered when someone at work behaved in a way that was familiar to him from years of observing and dealing with his sister. At times when he saw individuals "playing helpless" (his words), he stepped in so aggressively that his desire to challenge backfired and a minor issue became a major disruption for his relationship with the person. At other times, he would be triggered and react too harshly toward those whom he perceived were not observing appropriate boundaries. He described to Bridgette how in one instance, he gave a verbal dressing down to one of his direct reports whom he felt was inappropriately stepping in to

The key to a leader's ability to deal successfully with the poorly differentiated lies in understanding the reality of how such individuals function.

help a struggling intern from another division. As it turned out, he discovered after the fact that his direct report had been asked by HR to mentor the young man on a critical project.

Erik intuitively understood the wisdom of our Second Big Idea. But he needed help not only in managing his reactivity but also in understanding when it was important for him as a leader to step in and set boundaries and when he should keep quiet and let the other person learn from their own mistakes. The key, Bridgette explained, lies in understanding the reality of how a poorly differentiated person functions.

In Chapter 1 we introduced the notion of "differentiation of self" from Bowen Theory, and we offered a description of how a well-differentiated leader behaves. In subsequent chapters, we have been adding to that picture by fleshing out in each of the three Big Ideas some practical examples of what a resilient (i.e., well-differentiated) leader looks like. However, not every leader and not every person who works with or reports to a leader is well differentiated. In every organization, there are those who are poorly differentiated, and a resilient leader needs to recognize the characteristics of such individuals and deal with them in quite different ways than with others who have a higher level of differentiation.

Bridgette explained to Erik that a leader does not need a degree in clinical psychology to recognize certain characteristics of a poorly differentiated individual. The poorly differentiated can be spotted by two characteristics that are virtually always present: (1) emotional fusion in their relationships and (2) an inability to separate how they think from how they feel. Bridgette also shared with Erik some of the typical behaviors that leaders encounter in those who are poorly differentiated. Here are a few of them:

- They are not capable of self-regulation. They are easily triggered and highly reactive.
- They perpetually invade the space of others, intruding where they shouldn't and showing a lack of respect for others' boundaries.
- Their mistakes and mishaps are not their teachers; they fail to learn from their experiences.
- They don't accept responsibility for themselves and never see how they contribute to the conditions they complain about.

Because their behaviors are so invasive, and unless someone sets boundaries on those behaviors, these individuals inevitably infect the teams and organization with a higher level of anxiety, and they trigger reactivity in others. High performers get discouraged at the amount of energy required to deal with them, and their intensity has a magnifying effect on otherwise calm segments of the system.

Erik's Wins

Erik was learning to "think systems." He realized the negative effect the poorly differentiated can have on an entire organization and saw how important it was for him to learn more about how to recognize and deal effectively with such individuals. The happy ending to the story is that Erik had several wins as a result of the work he did with Bridgette. He recognized that far fewer people than he might have imagined truly needed him to function as their boundary setter. This improved his relationships with many people in his organization where he had been overfunctioning and relieved his overall stress level considerably.

He also worked on and made progress on self-management when his reactivity was triggered by the poorly differentiated few. He learned to put in place a number of best practices for dealing with his less differentiated employees, such as explicit meeting norms, greater clarity around policies and procedures and the consequences for failure to follow them, much more effort in developing position descriptions with roles and responsibilities spelled out, annual goal setting, and performance standards. Erik also established more intentional mechanisms to ensure consistent enforcement that held everyone accountable whenever any of these boundaries were breached.

Finally—and, for Erik, most important—he developed a much better understanding that his sister truly was not capable at this stage of her life of fully overcoming and owning her history of making poor choices and the impact of their parents' sincere but misguided parenting. She was very poorly differentiated, and he came to accept her for who she was. He also learned how to be more skillful in setting necessary boundaries with her without doing so in a reactive way. His more relaxed approach to dealing with her resulted in fewer "explosions" and even some relatively authentic experiences of sharing time with her at a deeper level.

Erik's story mirrors what many of our clients experience, which is that insights and growth in one area of life (i.e., on the home front) translate into greater effectiveness and capacity in another (i.e., their leadership impact at work).

STOP & REFLECT

- **Consider the people who currently report to you. Do any of them consistently display the characteristics of a poorly differentiated person as described above? If so, to what extent have you set and reinforced appropriate boundaries to limit their invasive tendencies?**

- **Do any of your family members, like Erik's sister, display the characteristics of poorly differentiated people? If so, to what extent have you set and reinforced appropriate boundaries to limit their invasive tendencies?**

Third Big Idea—A New Way of LEADING: Act as the "immune system" of the organization you lead.

We are all familiar with a bit of folk wisdom that is captured in slogans such as "no pain, no gain," or "what doesn't kill you makes you stronger." Our Third Big Idea builds on this familiar insight but focuses on what is required of a leader who wishes to "think systems" in applying this wisdom in a workplace setting.

Bridgette and Bob were training a group of newly appointed leaders, and among the participants was Grace, a young woman with a one-year-old who was expecting a second child in about four months. Grace was struggling with the challenges she was already facing as a new parent and knew that they would only multiply with the birth of a second child. On top of that, her recent promotion had placed her over an operating unit plagued by employee-related problems that would have been a test even for a seasoned leader.

Grace volunteered to share her situation as a case study for the group to discuss, and what came to light was that previous leaders in her firm had consistently failed to set boundaries or enforce accountability. The result was a laissez-faire culture that she knew needed to be addressed, but she was unsure how to go about it and was concerned she might not be up to the task. Like so many of her peers, she was convinced that leadership success required her to be compassionate and caring and to win over those she hoped would follow her lead. We presented our ideas around the fallacy of empathy as the framework for the case study and then facilitated a discussion between Grace and the other participants in the group. Eventually, Grace and the others were able to agree in theory to some strong measures that were needed to turn around the embedded culture, but many of them also admitted that they were not sure they would have the courage to take the kind of steps required.

In follow-up coaching with Bridgette, Grace had two breakthrough insights before going on maternity leave. When she returned to work following the birth, she resumed coaching and began implementing key aspects of a plan that eventually turned the culture around after several years.

Grace's Insights

The first breakthrough insight for Grace occurred when she and Bridgette reflected on how her young son was learning to walk and how important it was that she allow him to fall down and not always rush in to rescue him (despite the tears that often tug at a mother's heart). Bridgette shared her own experience as a mother of three and how difficult it had been for her (and is for every mother) to allow children to experience the painful consequences of their actions without shielding them, rescuing them, or even offering too much comfort. Children grow stronger and more resilient when their parents allow them to go through challenging, painful experiences, and they are helped to learn from those experiences when their parents display care but do not step in due to an excess of anxiety or empathy.

To do this, Grace realized, she needed to expand her capacity to tolerate the pain she saw in her children when they fell—literally or figuratively. She also needed to focus on her conviction that her children did, indeed, have within themselves everything that it took to pick themselves up from painful falls and go forward as stronger, more confident persons.

The second insight that was key to Grace's breakthrough was her grasp of the metaphor we shared with her that the leader of any organization acts as its "immune system" by challenging its members and by allowing them to undergo painful experiences that make them stronger and more resilient. Medical science has applied this insight to the development of vaccines. Our body's ability to fight off disease is strengthened, not weakened, when we successfully fight off toxic forces of all sorts. There is a natural resilience in our bodies and an innate capacity to learn from challenges, all in the interest of survival and healthy flourishing.

The leader of any organization acts as its "immune system" by challenging its members and by allowing them to undergo painful experiences that make them stronger and more resilient.

In the same way, it is the responsibility of leadership to strengthen an organization's "immune system"—its resilience—by increasing others' capacity to deal with challenges and pain. But—and this is the point that she realized was powerfully relevant to her both at home and at work—to accomplish this as a leader, Grace had to increase her threshold for the pain of others, whether they be her children or those she was responsible for leading in her operating unit. Her obligation was such that she could not afford to be overly sensitive—empathetic—to the sensitivities of those she was leading, lest their capacity for resilience be compromised.

Strategies for Leaders

Bridgette and Bob spoke with Grace several years later when they were doing further training in the organization, and she shared with them something else that she had only recently come to appreciate. The strategies she had put in place to turn around the laissez-faire culture of her unit were initially aimed primarily at those who were poorly differentiated and whose behaviors were egregious. But she was now aware that both the high performers and those who were good, steady workers had benefited from her decision to emphasize challenge more than comfort. At every level, she saw a stronger, more resilient organization that continued to thrive when encountering stretch goals, competitive threats, or other workplace challenges that once might have withered them. The key to her success, she said, was when she realized that she had to "toughen herself up" if she was going to be a better mom and unit leader. When asked what she would want to tell other leaders who needed to grow those same muscles, here's what she shared:

- Deepen your conviction that every person has a greater reservoir of strength and resiliency than meets the eye.
- Think deeply about why rescuing is not always the best impulse to follow.
- Watch your own reactivity in action, and practice pausing to consider thoughtfully before taking steps to fix someone's problem or lessen her/his pain.
- Watch for opportunities to practice in small ways the skill of letting others experience the consequences of their choices, especially when those consequences are painful for those you care about.
- Be intentional about reflecting on situations where empathy was not the best response. Write down your insights as a way of embedding them more deeply in your leadership repertoire.

Every leader who cares about the organization and the people that s/he leads—not to mention the other stakeholders who depend on the organization's success—wants to strengthen the organization's ability to remain healthy and flourish despite the challenges that threaten it. Threats will always exist, both within and without. This is true whether the leader is responsible for a family, a small nonprofit, a billion-dollar global company, or an entire nation. In every case, when the leader leads with a well-defined, thoughtful, and less anxious presence, the organization's odds of defending against the invasiveness of toxic forces are increased rather than lowered.

In the Conclusion (page 231), we offer some ideas about how you, as a more resilient leader, can promote greater resiliency in the systems you lead.

STOP & REFLECT

- **Think of a time when someone in your life increased your capacity to deal with challenges and pain. What did that person do, and how did his/her actions or words impact your development?**
- **How would you assess your current capacity to tolerate the discomfort and pain of others? To the extent that it might be needed, what could you do to grow this important leadership muscle?**

Core Practices

Ask What Is Most Needed

Next time an employee or family member is struggling or facing an important challenge, step back and reflect on the balance you are striking between *offering comfort* and *offering challenge*. Ask yourself what that person most needs (not wants) in order to grow stronger, and then adjust your behavior in the direction that is most appropriate.

Pause before Rescuing or Distancing

Next time someone important to you is struggling or facing an important challenge, notice if you are tempted to step in prematurely to rescue them from the pain or discomfort they may be feeling. Or, notice if you are tempted to distance yourself from the situation to avoid getting involved without carefully considering the capability of the person in light of the challenge they face. Think through, "I will step in only when it is really needed, not just because it is really wanted." Hit the pause button and practice increasing your tolerance for your own discomfort; remind yourself of the other person's inherent resilience.

Chapter Summary

- The *fallacy of empathy* refers to the mistaken belief that offering support, understanding, and comfort (especially to poorly differentiated others) will, by itself, promote greater responsibility for self.
- Learning to dispel this mistaken belief—in oneself and in the culture of the organization you lead—can be a powerful step toward building organizational health and resilience.
- Resilient leaders observe whether their default tendency is to offer comfort or to offer challenge, and they seek to strike a healthy balance between the two in light of what is most called for and appropriate to the situation at hand.
- A key skill for all leaders, but especially those who default to offering comfort, is to build their capacity for tolerating the pain and discomfort of others. Developing this "muscle" prevents them from stepping in too soon to fix others' problems or to rescue them from their pain.
- Statements like, "We are like family here" or "We have each other's back" can be indicative of a conflict-avoidant culture, reinforced by leaders who err too often on the side of offering comfort to those who struggle or underperform rather than challenging them to step up their game.
- In every family and every organization, there are poorly differentiated people who can and will invade the space of others if left unchecked. It is the leader's responsibility to establish and reinforce boundaries with such persons for the sake of preserving the overall health and integrity of the organization.
- Most people have within them greater reservoirs of strength and resiliency than they give themselves credit for. A resilient leader honors this reservoir and strengthens it by challenging those they lead to stretch and grow beyond their self-imposed limitations.

CHAPTER 9

CURIOSITY
HARNESSING YOUR LEADERSHIP SUPERPOWER

> The important thing is not to stop questioning.
> Curiosity has its own reason for existing.
>
> Albert Einstein

In earlier chapters of this book, we identified curiosity as a key ingredient in the practice of resilient leadership. In Chapter 1, we introduced the core practice of getting on the balcony, of which being curious is an essential component. In Chapter 2, we talked about bringing a "curious mindset" to meetings and conversations as a way of managing reactivity.

In this chapter, we intend to explore more deeply what curiosity is, how it works, and why it is essential to effective leadership and thriving organizations.

So what exactly is curiosity? The Cambridge Dictionary defines curiosity as *"an eager desire to know or learn about something."* It is an innate human quality, one that is easily observed in young children. Bridgette's 10-month-old grandson, Jayce, is the perfect embodiment of this definition. If you spend just five minutes in his presence, you will see that he's on a mission to understand and learn how *everything* works.

You can imagine what Jayce is thinking as he explores his environment: *"Hum… I wonder what will happen when I throw this ball at the dog?" "If I hammer the bookshelf, what noise will it make?" "How many bowls in this cupboard can I take out and slam on the ground?"*

One day as Jayce was sitting on the floor playing, he paused for a moment and held up his small hand in front of his face. He turned it over a few times, looking at it intently. *"What is this amazing thing here?"* he seemed to be wondering. He was truly captivated and in awe of his own hand!

Our hands are miraculous if you think about it. Throughout our lifetime, they are integral to so many facets of our human experience – holding hands with a loved one, stroking a beloved pet, creating a work of art, typing words that form a book, or making dinner for our families. And yet when was the last time you looked at your hands and marveled at their dexterity, ingenuity, or strength? As adults, our sense of wonder and awe can all too easily weaken. But the good news is that with practice, we can strengthen our curiosity muscle and aim it in any direction we want. And when we do, good things happen.

Two Kinds of Curiosity

Imagine the following scenario. You and your spouse are sitting on your deck reading one evening when an argument breaks out between the married couple who live next door. It starts with a slow burn but heats up quickly with harsh words being exchanged. Without thinking, you exchange glances with your spouse and then you both grow quiet and lean your heads towards the arguing couple. After all, inquiring minds want to know! What are they arguing about? Who is blaming whom for what? Did they really just say that?! A door slams and the argument is over, but your curiosity was definitely piqued. You exchange a few words with one another ("Wow, that was crazy!") and moments later you both return to reading your books.

This kind of curiosity is what author Judson Brewer, in his book, *Unwinding Anxiety,* calls **Deprivation Curiosity**. He defines it as the "Closed down, restless, need-to-know type – the itch that must be scratched." Once you know what you want to know, this curiosity is quenched and satisfied. Think of how restless you become when you hear your phone ping, alerting you to an incoming text message. *Who is that and what are they saying?* You feel compelled to pick up your phone just to ease that restless, need-to-know feeling, even if it means interrupting another more important task. It is easy to see how Deprivation Curiosity can lead to procrastination and distraction. In the workplace, it is the fuel behind grapevine gossip, spreading information and disinformation like wildfire. Part of a leader's job is to provide clarity when employees are experiencing Deprivation Curiosity and to satisfy it by communicating transparently and consistently.

In contrast, the kind of curiosity that Bridgette's grandson embodied is what Brewer refers to as **Interest Curiosity**, which he defines as the "Opened up, wide-eyed wonder of discovery." This kind of curiosity is motivated by a desire to learn something new and to solve problems in creative ways. It is not so much about *answering* questions, at least initially, as it is about *asking* them. Interest Curiosity is often accompanied by feelings of wonder and awe, and the human brain finds it deeply rewarding. In the workplace, leaders can cultivate Interest Curiosity by modeling it themselves and encouraging it in their teams.

Curiosity and Anxiety

In many respects, curiosity is an antidote to anxiety. In one study, participants who recounted a day they spent intentionally being curious boosted their mental and physical energy by 20% more than when they remembered a day on which they felt profound happiness. Being curious triggers the release of dopamine, which is the feel-good neurotransmitter responsible for pleasure. Dopamine enhances our sense of well-being, helps us to focus more, and increases our productivity. Curiosity is inherently rewarding, and it encourages us to explore further and discover more. When we are curious, we feel energized, enlivened, and hopeful. If you want a hit of dopamine-induced well-being, try adopting a curious mindset about something or someone. You may notice a shift in your mood and mental state.

However, the relationship between curiosity and anxiety is not a simple one. While curiosity feels good and is intrinsically rewarding, the discoveries it leads to can make us feel vulnerable. A major evolutionary task of our brains was to keep us safe from threats. Being vulnerable makes us feel threatened, leading to an increase in anxiety, at least in the short term. Suppose for example that you've decided to work with a leadership coach. Part of your engagement includes having 360-degree feedback collected from your peers and employees. You've been looking forward to getting the feedback, but when the morning of your 360 debrief arrives, you find yourself feeling some angst. You genuinely want to know how others see you, but what if significant blind spots are revealed? What if you disagree with the feedback or don't like what you hear? Your curious and open mindset is what led you to say yes to coaching and 360-degree feedback in the first place. And yet here you are now, feeling anxious!

Curiosity is inherently rewarding, and it encourages us to explore further and discover more.

Curiosity and discovery can be both exciting *and* anxiety-provoking. The process of growth is rarely a straight line. There are unforeseen twists and turns in almost any meaningful adventure, whether that adventure is a quest to better understand ourselves or to learn a new language. The good news is this: If we persist through the anxiety and discomfort that can be part of any novel or challenging learning experience – and bring our curious mindset to our discomfort – we increase our stress tolerance and our resilience.

Young children, like Bridgette's grandson Jayce, experience all of the rewards of curiosity and little of the accompanying anxiety. Unlike adults, they have yet to accumulate lasting memories of when their "opened up, wide-eyed wonder of discovery" was ultimately met with feelings of vulnerability or regret.

Our lived experiences can either bolster the curiosity and openness of our youth or dampen it, which leads to a wariness and play-it-safe mentality. This is why it behooves us to be intentional about practicing curiosity to reinforce its positive benefits, especially when it comes to our most important relationships with colleagues and family members. Busy with the never-ending demands of the day, we can lose that sense of wonder and curiosity about the people we live and work with, especially when those people confound and frustrate us. Reclaiming our innate curiosity helps us to see the people around us with fresh eyes. It also helps us to create brighter and more inspiring futures for ourselves and our teams.

STOP & REFLECT

- **When was the last time you experienced wonder and awe about something or someone? How did it feel? Did your curiosity lead to a new discovery or insight?**
- **Where does your curiosity shine most brightly these days? Are there certain subjects or areas of interest that you approach with wonder and awe? How about certain facets of your work?**

Curiosity as a Leadership Superpower

Curiosity not only triggers dopamine in our brains and makes us feel good; research has shown that it also has positive benefits for leaders and their organizations. A group of Harvard researchers – Claudio Fernandez-Araoz, Andrew Roscoe, and Kentaro Armaki – analyzed the development of leaders and found that curiosity is the best predictor of strength in seven key areas: results orientation, strategic orientation, collaboration and influence, team leadership, developing organizational capabilities, change management and market understanding. Their findings suggest a strong correlation between curiosity and leadership competence, especially when curious leaders are given developmental assignments that expose them to a variety of challenges, growth opportunities, and roles.

In our work as executive coaches, we have observed first-hand how curiosity benefits leaders. We have seen it deepen our clients' self-awareness and improve their ability to self-regulate; we have witnessed how curiosity turns our clients into better mentors and coaches; and we have watched how they model curiosity – by asking open and generative questions – and in doing so, spark innovation. And the benefits don't stop there. Leaders who embed curiosity into their workplace culture create learning organizations: workplaces where employees solve problems in creative ways, grow from their failures, and adapt to changing market conditions with agility.

Leaders who embed curiosity into their workplace culture create learning organizations.

Curiosity Enhances Self-Awareness and Self-Regulation

One of the core tenets of Resilient Leadership that we have explored in this book is the importance of becoming a more astute observer of ourselves. This means noticing how we are showing up and impacting others day-to-day, moment-to-moment, in all of our relationship systems – our families, the teams we are part of, and the organizations that we lead.

In our experience, one of the biggest impediments to deepening self-awareness and self-regulation is our tendency to judge ourselves and others harshly. We all possess an inner critic. Your inner critic may be especially hard on you, hard on others, or a little of both. Either way, this judgmental voice that constantly whispers in your ear can keep you from being open and vulnerable, both of which are pre-requisites for deep learning. This is where curiosity comes in.

Learning to observe ourselves with curiosity means being present to whatever is happening or has happened in an open and non-judgmental way. A good analogy would be how archeologists operate. They study excavation sites and the people who once lived there--not with judgment (e.g., "Why did these stupid people build these structures here?") but with respectful curiosity (e.g., "Hum, this is interesting. I wonder why these structures are here and why these people sacrificed so much to build them?").

When we observe ourselves (and others) with this kind of curiosity, it can transform the way we lead.

Dave's Story

Dave, a leader Bridgette once coached, was easily triggered by any signs of disrespect he detected in those he led, and he tended to see such people around every corner. As a result, he would overreact to challenges, even if they were well-intentioned, benign, and appropriate. His reactivity was something he was blind to, but those who interacted with him regularly clearly could see it.

Dave's trigger had its roots in his family of origin, where he had a bully for an older brother. The brother taunted Dave and had free reign to do so by the parents who regularly failed to recognize what was happening between the two siblings. Dave's brother was big and a gifted athlete, a combination that the family prized. Dave was small, not particularly coordinated, and was interested in music and the arts. He was also a gifted student but in a sports-loving family, he never got the acknowledgment or respect of his parents or brother, no matter how much he excelled in academics. Fast forward to the present, and Dave frequently reacted with anger and intensity to his employees--and even some of his clients--whenever they pushed back on his ideas or offered dissenting views. This created distance between him and the people he most needed for success—a source of much frustration and stress for Dave and his stakeholders.

In coaching, Dave gradually learned to be deeply curious about his reactions to triggering people and events. Instead of asking himself why he (or someone else) reacted so poorly, he would pause and say to himself, "Hum. That's interesting. I wonder what's really going on here?" He journaled about what triggered him, observed these incidents with a detached curiosity, and discovered for himself both the origins and the solution to his reactionary habit. The result not only brought him greater equanimity; it improved his relationships as well.

STOP & REFLECT

- **Think about a time when you were triggered by someone in a way that was surprising to you and perhaps disproportionate to the triggering event. How did you react and what was the impact?**
- **Bring a touch of curiosity to recalling this experience by asking yourself a few questions: What did this situation remind you of? Did you feel a core value was being disregarded? What assumptions did you make that you may not have been aware of? And lastly, how might you respond differently next time?**

Curiosity Turns Leaders into Better Coaches

Regardless of whether you are a supervisor, middle manager, or CEO, you probably started your career as an individual contributor. You developed expertise, became known for your ability to solve problems, and developed credibility by having the answers. When individual contributors become managers and leaders, their path to success changes. In today's volatile, complex world, no single leader can have all the answers. Instead, leaders need to harness the insights and ideas of those who work with them and for them. One powerful way to do that is by becoming a coach. Not the kind of external coach that Bridgette and Bob are, but rather by being a manager-as-coach who asks questions, listens genuinely, and guides employees to discover their own solutions.

Daniel Goleman, widely considered the father of emotional intelligence, identified the Coaching Leadership style as one of the most resonant and effective styles leaders can employ because of its positive impact on employee performance and productivity. It also enhances a leader's level of connection and trust with those they manage.

Sarah's Story

Sarah, a former client of Bob, was a successful VP of sales for a national organization. She reached out to him for help, explaining that she was feeling overwhelmed more often and needed to get a better sense of what needed to change in her priorities. She was excellent in her outward-facing role of finding new companies to pitch to, and she had a gift for uncovering her clients' unmet needs and then selling them on how her company's services could fulfill those needs. Bob knew that Sarah was intensely curious about her clients. She also asked them great questions and listened deeply to their responses. They in turn felt seen and heard.

But with her direct reports, it was a different story. Sarah believed her role as a manager was to solve problems and to provide answers to her employees' questions, which they brought to her often. Their endless requests for help were a major reason she was feeling overwhelmed and missing the part of her job she loved most – meeting with clients.

In one pivotal coaching session, Bob asked Sarah a question that caused her to grow silent for a long pause. "What if you started treating your direct reports more like you treat your clients?"

It did not take Sarah long to realize what Bob was suggesting. What if she aimed her curiosity at her direct reports, and asked questions that enabled them to discover for themselves the answers they were seeking? What if she talked less and listened more? This was the start of something new for Sarah. She and Bob brainstormed a list of questions she could have on hand when her employees came to her – questions like, "It sounds like you've been thinking about this for a while. What are some options you've thought about that might address this?" Or "What do you think is the most important next step you could take to make progress here?" She practiced asking questions from a place of genuine curiosity and listened more openly to her employees' responses. When needed, she would add her thoughts and guidance, but only after drawing out her employees' best thinking first.

Over a few months, her direct reports grew more capable and confident. They relied on Sarah's guidance less, but when they did seek her out, they were more prepared to bring their own best thinking to the conversation rather than rely on Sarah for hers. Becoming more of a manager-coach not only benefited her direct reports; it benefited Sarah as well. She grew to enjoy both aspects of her job – meeting with clients to uncover their needs and meeting with her direct reports to coach them toward greater self-competence and success. Best of all, Sarah's feelings of being overwhelmed were fewer and farther between.

What struck Bob most about Sarah's breakthrough was not that she got more curious, but rather that she was able to leverage her existing curiosity about clients and aim it in a new direction – toward her direct reports.

Who might you aim your curiosity towards more intentionally, and how might doing so benefit both you and them?

Curiosity Spurs Creativity and Innovation

Both Bridgette and Bob had the privilege of coaching many leaders during the pandemic and one thing became abundantly clear to us: The leaders with the most success were those who were able to face the uncertain future of a global pandemic with a potent blend of curiosity and optimism. At a time when others were despairing and stuck, these leaders approached the unfolding situation with an eye for opportunity. We could see the impact their calm confidence had on their employees – who also became curious and more confident in their ability to prevail. Rather than buckling under the weight of uncertainty and the disruption it created, their organizations seized the moment at hand and led with a lightness that belied the gravity of the times.

Ed Friedman taught that one of the hallmarks of an anxious family, team, or organization is the loss of laughter. Highly anxious people and organizations become deadly serious about themselves and their work. When the threat-detection system within our brains is on high alert, we tend to become tightly wound and more narrowly focused. This can be helpful in a true emergency that threatens our imminent safety. If a fire breaks out in our building or home, we need to be hyper-focused and ready to run, not making light of the threat with laughter!

An absence of laughter and playfulness not only sucks the joy out of work, it also stifles creativity and innovation.

But most of the problems we face in the workplace are less urgent than a fire alarm, and more complex and nuanced. They require our best, most creative thinking along with the contributions of others to solve. Collaborative problem-solving takes time, yet we often find ourselves seeking a quick fix under the influence of anxiety. If we are not mindful, our vision narrows, and our level of chronic anxiety rises--precisely at a time when we most need to be wide-eyed and open to discovery. An absence of laughter and playfulness not only sucks the joy out of work, it also stifles creativity and innovation.

Imagine for a moment two meetings, at two different companies, taking place at the same time during the height of the pandemic. Both organizations are manufacturing companies facing novel challenges that could ultimately put their company out of business.

In one meeting, the mood is somber. The kind of questions being asked are anxiety laced, and not particularly generative or helpful. Questions like, *"What will happen if we have to shut down and lay off employees?"* And *"How will we survive if we can't produce our products?"* The ensuing discussion is laden with untested assumptions and lacks both clarity and creativity. People leave in a dark mood and drained of energy.

In the other meeting, at another company, the conversation is quite different. The seriousness of the situation is acknowledged, but the leader is helping the team to look at things from a variety of angles and through a wider lens. Questions are asked from a place of curiosity, not fear, and are more generative. Questions like, *"What might we do, now and in the next three months, to ensure our long-term survival?"* And *"How can we keep the factory open, and put in place rigorous safety measures to protect employees?"* The discussion is fruitful with several new ideas surfacing. It concludes with a commitment to move forward with a revamped system for producing the company's main product – a change that had stalled before the pandemic but which is now being enthusiastically embraced. Despite the gravity of the discussion, the end of the meeting is punctuated with a moment of shared laughter, lightening the mood and the way forward.

The latter conversation is an example of the kind of successful meetings that Bridgette and Bob frequently witnessed as they coached various leaders and their teams during the pandemic. Asking questions from a place of wonder and curiosity was a core practice for these teams and often their first step toward innovation. Resilient organizations provide a powerful reminder of a simple truth: Nothing new gets created – in our teams or our organizations – unless and until we lean in, get curious, and ask different questions.

STOP & REFLECT

- **What questions are you asking yourself and your team these days? As you consider your questions, notice with curiosity if they are generative, energizing and inspiring. If not, how might you re-frame them?**
- **When was the last time you heard laughter erupt in your team? If the answer is too long ago to remember, how might introducing a more curious, even playful mood, help you and your team to tackle current challenges more creatively?**

Creating a Culture of Curiosity

When we are curious, we are more likely to pay attention to new information and to remember it better. This is because curiosity activates the hippocampus, a key part of the brain that is involved in memory formation and learning.

Neuroscience has widely researched and documented the role curiosity plays in enhancing our ability to learn. Curiosity is not only pivotal in helping individuals to learn, but it also plays an instrumental role in creating learning organizations. Such organizations have a culture of curiosity, where leaders at all levels model curiosity and inquisitiveness. These leaders actively encourage employees to explore innovative ideas and support them when they take bold, calculated risks. According to Deloitte, organizations with a learning culture have shown to be 92% more likely to develop novel products and processes, are 52% more productive, and are 17% more profitable compared to organizations that fail to promote a learning culture.

Cultivating a culture of curiosity and learning also paves the way for greater employee engagement. Novartis, a global healthcare company based in Switzerland, has committed considerable time and resources to embedding curiosity and learning into its workplace culture. Research across industries has shown that having an opportunity to learn is one of the top reasons people join an organization. Wanting to do even better at talent acquisition and retention, Novartis investigated the barriers to learning within their own company and found that a lack of time and a lack of support from managers were the key barriers. To combat this, they set an aspiration that all employees spend 5% of their time – or a hundred hours a year --- learning, building their skills, and being curious. Novartis has also committed to developing leaders at all levels who model curiosity with their teams. To see what difference such leaders make, they studied employee engagement scores across the company. Results of the study clearly showed that the main difference between leaders with high employee engagement levels and those with lower levels was the leader's curiosity. The bottom line? Poor leaders stifle curiosity, great leaders promote it, boost employee engagement, and create the culture required for teams to excel.

The main difference between leaders with high employee engagement levels and those with lower levels was the leader's curiosity.

STOP & REFLECT

- **To what extent does your workplace culture value and reward curiosity and learning?**
- **How well is curiosity being modeled by leaders at all levels in your organization? To what extent are you modeling curiosity and openness with your team?**

Core Practices

The benefits of a culture of curiosity for leaders and their organizations are numerous and compelling. But how do we go about practicing it, if we want to bring more curiosity to our leadership and life?

We have found that specificity makes any practice our clients undertake more likely to happen and therefore more successful. With that in mind, here are three suggestions you might find helpful:

1) **Pick a specific relationship you want to improve.** This might be someone you have grown distant from, someone with whom you tend to have conflict, or someone you do not currently understand very well. Practice bringing more of a curious mindset to your interactions with this person. Pay attention to the assumptions and judgments you make about them and whether you treat them as facts. Make a point to show up in your conversations with a bit less judgment (as in, *"I can't believe they feel this way!"*) and a bit more "wonder" (as in, *"Hmmm, I wonder why this person might be feeling this way."*).

2) **Pick a specific meeting that you attend regularly**, but which you find boring, contentious or challenging. Bring a curious mindset to the next several meetings you attend. Observe how present you are during the meeting as well as the mood you typically bring to it. Be intentional about asking more open-ended questions and listening more deeply. Notice the difference it makes, either in how you feel about the meeting or your contribution to it.

3) **Pick a specific employee you manage,** perhaps one that isn't performing up to the standards you know or believe they are capable of. For your next several meetings with this employee, practice asking different questions from a deeply curious place. Talk less, listen more, and be open to what you learn.

Curiosity and Differentiation

In Chapter 1, we introduced the notion of differentiation, a concept developed by Murray Bowen and then applied to leaders and their organizations by his protégé, Ed Friedman. One of the foundations of this book is our conviction that the higher a leader's level of differentiation, the greater that leader's capacity for effective leadership.

Well-differentiated leaders stand apart from the emotional pressures of the day while still staying powerfully connected to others. They make decisions based on clear principles rather than on what is popular or expedient. When faced with uncertainty and change, they lead boldly and with conviction, yet they remain open to the input of others, even when that input challenges their thinking and tests their assumptions. Every team and organization craves a well-differentiated leader, and in today's VUCA world, such leaders are needed now more than ever.

In our Resilient Leadership training programs, we emphasize the three foundational building blocks of a well differentiated leader: self-awareness, self-definition and self-regulation. We hope this chapter makes clear the connection between curiosity and differentiation. After all, it is impossible to define who we are, to regulate our anxiety in the face of anxious others, or to become more self-aware without curiosity! A curious, open mindset is what fuels the lifelong journey towards greater differentiation and growth. As such, it is a vital part of being an effective leader and an indispensable part of a life well-lived.

Chapter Summary

- Every moment we spend being deeply curious about something or someone triggers the release of dopamine, the brain's feel-good chemical. Curiosity makes us happier, more focused, and more productive. In this way, a habit of curiosity is an antidote to chronic anxiety.
- When our curiosity leads to discoveries that make us feel vulnerable, we can experience an increase in anxiety, at least in the short term. But when we bring a curious mindset to our discomfort and stay the course despite it, we increase our tolerance for stress and our resilience in the face of it.
- The hippocampus is the part of the brain associated with memory and learning. Being curious activates this region of the brain, improving the acquisition and retention of new learnings.
- Not all forms of curiosity are created equal. The "opened-up, wide-eyed wonder of discovery" which Judson Brewer calls "Interest Curiosity", is the kind of curiosity that benefits leaders and organizations the most.
- Learning Organizations, which are based on a culture of curiosity, are more productive, innovative, and profitable.
- Curiosity enhances self-awareness and self-regulation, turns leaders into better coaches, and provides the spark for innovation. It is also positively correlated with leadership competence and employee engagement.
- Our life experience often dampens the curiosity of our youth, especially when it comes to our relationships. Long-standing patterns of reactivity can settle in and become the status quo. Bringing curiosity to the relationships that matter most to us is a powerful way to leverage this innate gift and enliven those relationships.

CHAPTER 10

THE NEUROSCIENCE OF RESILIENT LEADERSHIP
NEW INSIGHTS OPENING NEW POSSIBILITIES

The brain is the most adaptable organ in the human body.

—Norman Doidge
The Brain that Changes Itself

Twelve years ago, Bridgette and Bob were hired to provide coaching to a group of senior leaders at a fast-paced high-tech start-up company. The coaching engagement kicked off with a group meeting to introduce the coaches, outline how the coaching process works, and answer any questions the participants might have. We also decided to end the meeting by introducing the practice we call "6 Second Centering." You might recall this practice from Chapter 2. The act of centering helps leaders calm their nervous system and lower their anxiety, which in turn enables them to embody greater poise under pressure.

Having made it this far in the book, you may have already adopted 6 Second Centering as one of your own practices or perhaps you think it is something that many leaders would find valuable to learn. However, for the senior leaders we met with, this was definitely not the case. The first part of the meeting went well, and a general feeling of openness characterized the discussion. But as Bob began to introduce 6 Second Centering, the mood in the room significantly shifted. Bridgette noticed a few of the participants rolling their eyes, and a couple of them even started to quietly, but noticeably, laugh! When Bob finished leading them through the practice and tried to debrief it with them, an awkward silence descended on the room. Clearly, the practice didn't resonate with this group of hard-charging leaders.

Today we teach 6 Second Centering to large audiences of leaders and nearly all of them are not only receptive and eager to learn it but find it to be one of the most useful things they take away from our training and coaching programs.

What's Going On Here?

The difference in receptivity from a dozen years ago to today is not that leaders have become any less hard-charging or busy. In fact, they are busier than ever! The difference lies in the pivotal role neuroscience findings and concepts like emotional intelligence are playing in shaping our understanding of how the human brain functions and the implications this shared understanding has for the workplace.

Twelve years ago, when the above meeting took place, familiarity with emerging neuroscience was relatively scarce in the business community (and in some ways, it still is today) and recognition of the value of emotional intelligence for leadership effectiveness was just gaining traction. While we had a lot of anecdotal evidence and considerable social science research to back up our claims, we didn't have a great deal of neuroscience findings at our fingertips. Today, we are better at explaining why certain leadership practices work, and why others don't, based on a rapidly increasing volume of solid neuroscience research.

The application of neuroscience to the art of leadership is evolving at breathtaking speed.

Throughout this book, we have offered several neuroscience tidbits that help ground various practices in the Resilient Leadership toolkit. The application of neuroscience to the art of leadership is evolving at breathtaking speed, and new research is being done all the time. Those new findings have and will continue to inform our work and the practice of Resilient Leadership. The purpose of this chapter is to share a sampling of the neuroscience findings we have come across since writing the first edition of this book, particularly those that have proven most helpful to leaders seeking to practice Resilient Leadership, both at work and at home.

Five Neuroscience Findings to Help You Lead (Yourself and Others) More Effectively

1. Your Brain is a Neural Network that Rewires Itself Throughout Your Lifetime

Bob once coached a client who was 62 years old and very successful in his chosen field. While conducting a series of 360-degree feedback interviews for his client, Bob noticed among those he interviewed a general skepticism about his client's willingness and ability to change. More than one person said some version of, "You can't teach an old dog new tricks" or "He's not going to change. He's been at this a long time and the way he does things is hard-wired into him." Some of this skepticism was due to a perceived lack of this leader's openness to change. But some of the skepticism was also due to the widely held common belief that at his age, making substantive change was not likely and maybe not even possible – his way of doing things was "hard-wired" into him.

So, can you really teach an old dog new tricks? Fortunately, this question no longer needs to be a matter of opinion. Instead, we can turn to recent neuroscience findings for insight and answers.

Neuroplasticity, a term that has found its way into popular vernacular, refers to the brain's ability to change and adapt. Neuroscientists have been studying this for years. Yet new research into the brain's functioning has revealed that the brain is even more adaptable and flexible than we had previously thought and that it keeps growing and changing throughout our lifetime, even up to our death.

In his book, *Live Wired: The Inside Story of the Ever-Changing Brain,* neuroscientist David Eagleman paints a picture of the human brain as a vast, complex neural network of connectivity and flexibility. This neural network is continuously reshaping itself in response to our experience, through a process called synaptic pruning – the strengthening of frequently used neural connections and the weakening or elimination of unused ones. This continuous reshaping of our brain through synaptic pruning is what enables us to learn new skills, adapt to new environments, improve our cognitive functioning as we age, and even recover from brain injury – by rerouting damaged pathways and forming new connections to restore interrupted functioning.

Fortunately, it isn't just extraordinary events like a brain injury, that reshape our brain. Every experience we have, from the mundane to the extraordinary, leaves its mark on our brains. According to Eagleman, neuroplasticity is a function of not only what happens to us, *but what we choose to do.* When we choose to learn a complex skill like a new language, for example, it changes our brain in very specific ways. After learning a second language, bilingual individuals have more grey matter in several areas of their brains including the singular cortex (a key area for decision-making) and the basal ganglia (involved in managing emotions).

New research into the brain's functioning has revealed that the brain is even more adaptable and flexible than we had previously thought.

But we don't have to enroll in a foreign language course or learn a new skill to reshape our brain. Neuroscience research shows that the brain can also change as a result of a simple yet profound choice we make on a daily basis – namely, where we decide to focus our attention. The act of shifting who and what we pay attention to when done consistently, reshapes the brain's neural network by forming and strengthening new synaptic connections. As one of Bridgette's mentors, Richard Strozzi-Heckler, often says, *"Whatever we pay attention to grows larger in our lives."* From a neuroscience perspective, this is literally true.

Stop & Reflect

- **According to Eagleman, "*Neuroplasticity means that we are never finished products. We are always works in progress, forever capable of learning and growing.*" To what extent do you think of yourself, or the people around you, as "works in progress, forever capable of growing"?**
- **What examples do you have in your own life of your brain's neuroplasticity? How have you reshaped your own brain through practicing a new behavior, learning a new skill, or simply deciding to shift your focus and what you pay attention to? How might you do more of this?**

The good news is that neuroplasticity is ongoing throughout our lifetime. Research shows that our brains remain malleable into old age and can even improve in some areas with specific effort and activities. Several studies (cited by the Journal of Psychology and Aging and the National Institutes for Aging) show that older adults who learn to play and practice video games experience an increase in their cognitive functioning in key areas including reaction time, attention, memory, and global cognition. The suggested "Core Practices" at the end of each chapter of this book build on this insight.

In some ways, our brains may even become wiser as we age. According to a recent film on neuroplasticity by *The Economist*, in middle age, our brains learn to minimize the negative. Scientists have found that the amygdala, an area of the brain that deals with emotions, lights up on fMRI scans when younger people look at both positive and negative images. But for older adults, the brain (and the amygdala in particular) is much less reactive when shown negative images. Decades of dealing with difficult situations and life events make the older adult brain more efficient and more resilient in the face of adversity.

So, back to the question, can you really teach an old dog new tricks? From a neuroscience standpoint, the answer is unequivocally "YES"!

Your brain is constantly transforming itself right up until you take your last breath, and you can play an active role in ensuring it does just that. According to Irena O'Brien, a neuroscientist and founder of the Neuroscience Institute, if you want to promote ongoing change in your brain and behavior, three important ingredients are required: a clear goal, deliberate effort, and sustained repetition over time.

It turns out that coaching, which includes all three of these ingredients, may be one of the best ways to do just that.

2. Coaching Can Help You Rewire Your Brain

We have long advocated for including coaching with our training programs because the statistics about retention of learning are unequivocal – participants who attend a training program coupled with coaching retain significantly more than those who attend that same training program without the benefit of coaching. In one study, training plus coaching led to an increase of 82% in productivity versus 22% from training alone.

Why is this? Coaching helps people to set clear goals and intentions for change and then focuses on helping people practice new ways of thinking and behaving to achieve those goals and aspirations. Repeated practice of new ways of thinking and behaving reshape our brains through the process Eagleman describes in his book – synaptic pruning. Our Resilient Leadership training and coaching programs include several core practices for this very reason.

Repeated practice of new ways of thinking and behaving reshape our brains through the process of synaptic pruning.

When we introduce those practices, we are fond of saying, "We become what we practice," (a sentiment first expressed by Aristotle). From a neuroscience point of view, this is not just a figurative or metaphorical statement; it is quite literally true. A coaching relationship provides a powerful accountability structure characterized by trust, rather than coercion. The personalized reinforcement offered by a coach is an ideal mechanism to support the application of learning from a training experience.

Studies are also revealing that in addition to promoting lasting behavior change, modalities like therapy – and by extension coaching – actually reshape the brain's functioning in ways that decrease anxiety, lessen reactivity, and lower depression.

A recent meta-analysis of 17 research studies focused on how the brains of patients changed following psychological therapy. Two key findings seem relevant to the value of coaching: The first was that amygdala activity decreased following therapy. The amygdala is a region of the brain involved in processing emotions including fear and anxiety and is also involved in triggering the fight or flight response. The second finding was that following therapy patients showed a decrease in activation in the left precentral gyrus, an area of the prefrontal cortex involved in rumination and worrying, another key feature of depression.

Coaching is not therapy, and the kind of rigorous scientific study of the effects of therapy on the brain have not been repeated for coaching. But since all behavior change is brain change, it seems fair to suggest that coaching likely reshapes areas of the brain in similar ways to therapy. Both help people to change negative thinking patterns, and both help people to behave in new ways through repeated practice, leading to greater emotional self-regulation, lower levels of anxiety, and decreased rumination and worry. The ability to self-regulate one's emotions and be a less anxious presence is at the heart of what it means to be a resilient leader

The bottom line is this: insight alone does not create lasting change in the brain, but insight followed by deliberate practice does. The implication for leaders is clear. If you want to promote greater resilience and achieve lasting change – either in yourself or in those you lead – consider making coaching (whether done internally by managers or externally by professional coaches) a part of your training and development initiatives. The study referenced above that documented an 82% increase in productivity provides a strong endorsement for wedding training and coaching when the aim is to maximize the return on your investment and to provide a greater chance for lasting change.

3. Your Brain Treats Uncertainty as a Threat – Clarity Calms it Down

In Chapter 2, we talked about how a lack of clarity in the rational system provokes reactivity in the emotional system. We also emphasized how a leader's clarity of vision, values, and principles is a calming force in an anxious system.

Since we wrote that chapter, we have experienced a global pandemic as well as a host of other highly disruptive events that have brought the level of uncertainty we experience daily to a new level. How can leaders provide clarity in this increasingly uncertain world? And, from a neuroscience perspective, why does this matter? The answer to these questions lies in understanding how uncertainty impacts our brains.

The human brain craves certainty and this bias is strongly linked to the brain's predictive-making capabilities and preferences. David Rock, author and founder of the NeuroLeadership Institute, states, *"Like an addiction to anything, when the craving for certainty is met, there is a sensation of reward that occurs within the brain… It's part of the reason games like solitaire, Sudoku, and crossword puzzles are enjoyable. They give you a little rush from creating more certainty in the world in a safe way."*

Just about everything we do daily involves using memories from our past experiences, along with sensory information we are receiving in the present, to predict current and future events. Making predictions is the neocortex's primary function and is one of the ways our brain helps us to navigate and make sense of the world. Uncertainty is perceived as threatening precisely because it interferes with our brain's prediction-making capabilities and the neuro-chemical "rush" it gives us when we get it right. We may live in an uncertain world, but that doesn't stop our brain from craving certainty.

While leaders often are not able to provide the kind of certainty that their followers crave, the good news is that clarity is a very good substitute. When leaders are clear (even when they don't have all the answers) it helps them calm the nervous systems of their followers, reducing their sense of threat, and paving the way for them to maintain better focus and increase productivity.

John's Story

As the pandemic began to wind down, one of Bridgette's clients was struggling to decide when and how to bring employees back to the office. Like many leaders at this time, John and his executive team were not in alignment about how many days in the office they should require of employees. John wanted employees back in the office full-time, while his team expressed concerns about the number of employees that might leave if such a decision were to be made. While he and his team debated the issue, the employees became increasingly anxious.

The lack of information, and the uncertainty it created, began to impact employee morale and productivity. John was aware of this, but he felt he had to delay his communication until he knew exactly what his decision would be. As he shared with Bridgette, "I don't want to tell employees one thing, only to turn around and contradict myself a few weeks later."

But when Bridgette was able to share with John the impact of uncertainty on the brain and why his employees craved certainty, John realized it was a mistake to keep putting off any communication about the current thinking among him and his leadership team. While he still didn't have a complete answer, John decided he would schedule a meeting with all his employees and share what he could with them.

During that meeting, John admitted he and his leadership team had been struggling with the decision and that it was a hard one for him to make. After all, he knew he wasn't going to make everyone happy, no matter what he decided. He also made it clear that while he didn't yet know how many days a week employees would be required to be in the office, he could say with certainty that coming back five days a week was off the table. John shared the reasoning behind his desire for a hybrid solution – he believed being in person some days of the week was essential to preserving their culture of collaboration. Lastly, he told them he would make the decision with input from his executive team, and he promised to communicate that decision by the end of the month.

When John finished speaking, a collective feeling of relief was tangible in the room. While not everyone was certain to get their preferred outcome, at least they knew the current status of the issue and when it would be finally resolved.

What's Going on Here?

John's initial reluctance to communicate with his organization was based on a false assumption that certainty and clarity are one and the same. They aren't. Leaders can provide clarity even when they don't have all of the answers their followers are looking for. Here are the key ingredients John used to lower anxiety among his employees:

Be transparent ("This is a hard decision for me to make and I've been struggling with it.")

Eliminate as many outcomes as possible ("I can say with certainty that we won't require your presence in the office 5 days a week.")

Share how and when decisions will be made ("I will be making this decision with input from the executive team and will communicate this decision by the end of the month.")

Reiterate your values and guiding principles ("I believe that coming back to the office for part of the week is essential to preserving our culture of collaboration.")

If leaders can remember that uncertainty is highly threatening to the human brain, they can use this knowledge to their advantage. Instead of waiting to be clear once all the answers and decisions have been made, they can take the time to provide more clarity along the way. In an increasingly uncertain world, clarity is the new certainty.

Stop & Reflect

- **Is there a decision you are struggling to make that could be creating uncertainty for your team or organization? If so, how might this be impacting them?**
- **Which of the ingredients above might you be able to share with your team, even though you may not have all the answers right now about exactly how you will ultimately move forward?**

4. Your Nervous System is Inextricably Connected to the Nervous Systems of Other People

As we previously said, our brains are constantly being re-wired throughout our lives, not only by the events that happen to us but by our own choices and actions. What is equally true is that other human beings around us – our colleagues, friends, family members, and even strangers to some extent – also re-wire our brains, and we have the same effect on them. This process, known as co-regulation, happens beneath conscious awareness.

We tend to think that our highly developed human brains set us apart from the entire animal kingdom and that we are radically different from the "lower" species whose brains lack our complex abilities. It is certainly true that our ability to reason and reflect, to imagine future possibilities, and to engage in abstract thought set us apart from the vast majority of life forms with whom we share planet Earth.

But the greater truth is that in most ways, we are not all that different from our evolutionary ancestors who, like us, are highly social creatures. We use the term "instinct" to describe a huge range of abilities that manifest the deep connections that exist between the brains and the behaviors among virtually every non-human species. We've watched videos of vast herds of wildebeests grazing on the African savannah reacting simultaneously to an unseen threat, signaling to one another in some mysterious, unseen way, to flee from a stalking predator. We watch in awe at the murmuration of a huge flock of starlings, moving in one large mass across the evening sky, in a synchronized swooping and aerial dance whose precision and complexity makes a mockery of humans locked in rush-hour traffic jams below.

> **"It's a biological fact that humans have socially dependent nervous systems, which means your words affect other peoples' bodies and brains."**

Co-regulation is evidence of the profoundly social nature of our nervous systems, a phenomenon that we share widely with all earthly life forms. This is the biological foundation for the fact that changes in one person's body can prompt changes in another person's body, whether they are aware of it or not, and this happens regardless of whether they are friends, colleagues, or strangers coming together for the first time.

Research has discovered that when we are in conversation with others, for example, our breathing can synchronize as can the beating of our hearts. This is true whether the interaction is a casual one or a heated argument.

In her book, *Seven and a Half Lessons About the Brain,* neuroscientist and researcher Lisa Feldman Barret states, "It's a biological fact that humans have socially dependent nervous systems, which means your words affect other peoples' bodies and brains. If you raise your voice or even your eyebrows, you can affect what goes on inside other peoples' bodies, such as their heart rate or the chemicals carried in their bloodstream. If your loved one is in pain, you can lessen her suffering by simply holding her hand."

And we don't even need to be physically present to impact one another with our words. When you text an encouraging message to a loved one who lives far away, for example, their blood pressure lowers and their oxytocin levels rise, as does yours (oxytocin is the bonding hormone that helps us to feel safe and connected).

As a social species that lives and works together, this co-regulation has significant implications. Studies show that when your words or actions have a positive impact on other peoples' bodies and brains, they are less likely to get sick, more likely to trust and collaborate with others, and even experience improved health outcomes. And the reverse is true. When your actions and words impact other peoples' bodies and brains negatively, especially on a repeated or frequent basis, they are more likely to get sick, gain weight, and experience burnout.

"Your nervous system is bound up with the behavior of other humans, for better and worse."

As Feldman says, "Your nervous system is bound up with the behavior of other humans, for better and worse. The best thing for your nervous system is another human. The worst thing for your nervous system is also another person."

For this reason, it behooves us to be mindful of the signals we are sending, overtly through our words and behavior, and covertly through the functioning of our nervous system. It has often been said that the best gift a leader or parent can give their team or family is a well-regulated nervous system. Feldman's research helps us to understand why at a deeper level.

Stop & Reflect

- **Think of a time recently when a colleague, family member, or stranger impacted your nervous system, either by raising your cortisol levels and heart rate (inducing stress) or by increasing your oxytocin levels (inducing connection and trust). What did they say or do and how did it impact you?**
- **Think of a time when your words and actions (as a leader or a parent) impacted the nervous system of those around you (as evidenced by their reaction to you). Was the impact you had positive or negative?**
- **What helps you to regulate your nervous system such that it is a gift to those you live with and lead?**

5. Your Brain Creates Anxiety Through Two Pathways

When people are asked why they are stressed or anxious, they often cite something happening that is external to them as the source – an event, circumstance, or person that is causing their anxiety or stress. If only that person or situation would change, they would be less anxious! There is some truth to this because as we just discussed, there is a constant, mutual interaction between our nervous system and that of others with whom we interact. But when we peek inside the brain and see what is happening when people get anxious, a more complete, complex picture emerges, including the role that our brains play in the level of anxiety we experience. From a neuroscience perspective, anxiety is created in the brain and originates in either the amygdala or the cerebral cortex. Understanding this fact can help us to better manage our anxiety, whether it is being influenced by the actions of another person or is arising internally, from our anxiety-producing thoughts.

The Amygdala Pathway

Imagine being awakened in the middle of the night by a loud banging noise. You are home alone and the noise is foreign and menacing. You sit up abruptly, grab your phone, and dial 911, sure that an intruder has broken into your home. Your heart is pounding, your breath is rapid, and you can feel the palms of your hands becoming clammy. The threat detection system in your brain is on full alert until you realize moments later that the loud noise is coming from a large tree branch outside being blown against your bedroom window. Relieved, you hang up the phone and as you take some deep breaths, your nervous system begins slowly but surely to settle down.

What's going on here?

Amygdala-based anxiety begins with sensory information coming into the brain (in this case in the form of a loud banging noise), where it is received by the thalamus, which is like the "Grand Central Station" of the brain. The thalamus directs sensory information to various parts of the brain. In this example, the sensory information is sent directly to the amygdala, which activates the fight or flight response. Detecting a threat, a cascading cocktail of chemicals is released into the body including cortisol, the stress hormone. The benefit of the amygdala pathway is the remarkable speed at which it operates, which can be a lifesaver when we are dealing with urgent, immediate dangers. Within seconds, our body is equipped to fight, flee, or freeze, depending on what is called for in the circumstance.

While it helps us to survive, amygdala-based anxiety sometimes operates like a faulty alarm system, as it did in the example above, flooding our bodies with stress-inducing neurochemicals even in the absence of a real threat. The amygdala pathway is the major contributor to acute anxiety – what we define as *a transient state of unease in the face of an immediate threat.* Over time, the effects of acute anxiety (triggered more readily and more frequently by the VUCA world we live in) can add up, eroding our health, our immune system, and our well-being.

Fortunately, there are proven ways to manage amygdala-based anxiety and mitigate its impact. Anything we do that intervenes in the physiology of the stress response can help. 6 Second Centering, which we introduced in Chapter 2, is one such practice. Other strategies our clients find helpful include regular practice of meditation, taking deep breaths, prayer, listening to music, and being outside in nature.

Exercise and a good night's sleep have a powerful effect on calming the amygdala.

A variety of neuroimaging studies, cited in *Rewire Your Anxious Brain* by Catherine Pitman and Elizabeth Karle, show that the amygdala can be strongly impacted (for better or for worse) by our levels of both sleep and exercise. A good night's rest can settle a jittery amygdala, while several nights of poor sleep can make our amygdala more prone to sensing threats around every corner. Exercise, which many of our clients use regularly to manage the inherent stressors in their jobs, has a powerful effect on calming the amygdala and is more effective in doing so than many anti-anxiety medications.

Lastly, identifying your triggers – the range of stimuli (people and situations) that provoke the stress response in you – and working to change your automatic reactions to them, is probably one of the most powerful strategies you can employ. Our body's immune system learns to recognize a variety of toxins and over the years builds up defenses to neutralize them. In much the same way, recognizing how toxic situations (and people) make us more anxious allows us to thoughtfully plan how we will neutralize or at least manage them to lower their impact on us. You can learn more about how to identify your triggers and retrain your brain's reactions to them by consulting "How to Tame Your Triggers" in the Appendix on page 258.

The Cortex Pathway

We've all had those nights when we struggle in vain to fall asleep. Imagine an evening in which despite going to bed early, you find yourself tossing and turning and unable to sleep. You are safe and secure in your bed (no signs of an intruder on this night), yet you feel an abiding state of unease. Your monkey mind is swirling with unsettling thoughts and concerns that you can't seem to let go of. You recall a comment that a family member made earlier in the evening, which now seems to loom larger and feels more unsettling in the dark of night. You begin to project some of these thoughts and concerns into the future, and soon you find yourself imagining vivid details that convince you of an inevitable, negative outcome. The more you dwell on these nocturnal fantasies, the more real they seem. And the more real they seem, the more trouble you have relaxing into sleep. You roll over and check your clock for the third time that evening; it's 3 am, and sleep feels more elusive than ever.

What's going on here?

The cortex is an area of the brain that – at its best – helps us to think logically, interpret events, imagine future possibilities, and solve problems creatively. These are powerful capabilities that are helpful in many circumstances. However, in the above example, your cortex's ability to imagine possibilities and interpret events is the culprit that escalates your anxiety. In the middle of a sleepless night, your cortex created a threatening scenario that didn't exist and would likely never come to be. This interpretation of a negative future then activated your amygdala, which in turn triggered a low-grade, cortisol-fueled stress response. With a racing mind and elevated heart rate, along with tightening of your muscles, no wonder you couldn't sleep!

The cortex pathway described above is the main contributor to what we call chronic anxiety – an abiding state of unease *in the face of imagined or anticipated threats.* While the cortex in our example is a source of anxiety, that is not always how it functions. Our cortex also has amazing powers of logical reasoning, problem-solving, and positive imagination that can help calm anxiety and promote greater thoughtfulness. Whether it is a source of anxiety or a calming force for good depends in large part on how we choose to engage with this part of our brain.

Our cortex also has amazing powers of logical reasoning, problem-solving, and positive imagination that can help calm anxiety.

One of the best strategies we can use to manage the cortex pathway is a practice we call "Getting on the Balcony" which we introduced in Chapter 1. This involves taking a step back from the immediacy of an anxiety-producing situation or interpretation and using curiosity to engage our cortex in what it does best – thinking creatively and holistically about how to move past obstacles and create the future we desire.

We can also combat cortex-based anxiety by learning to develop a healthy skepticism for the worrisome thoughts and scary future scenarios our brains generate. We too easily treat our anxious thoughts, concerns, and interpretations as if they were facts, failing to challenge them and the assumptions they are based upon. But, if we understand the connection between cortex-based negative thinking and its activation of our amygdala, we can be more intentional about adopting a curious – rather than anxious – focus. Get on the balcony, breathe deeply, take six seconds to center yourself, observe your thinking with curiosity (and perhaps skepticism), and deliberately relax your tight muscles.

So, the next time you are feeling anxious and are tempted to blame it solely on an outside event, another person, or a difficult situation, pause to consider the active role that your brain – either your amygdala, your cortex, or both – is playing in generating and sustaining your anxiety. Then pick one of the strategies we've mentioned above that works for you and employ it. Doing so will make all the difference.

Chapter Summary

- Neuroplasticity refers to the brain's ability to re-wire itself by a process known as synaptic pruning. While neuroscientists have known about this capability for some time, new research reveals that our brain is even more adaptable than had been previously thought.
- Your brain's plasticity lasts into old age, with studies showing that even older brains can be reshaped through intentional practice, resulting in some cases in improved cognitive functioning.
- Life events shape your brain but so do your own choices and day-to-day actions. The simple act of choosing to shift your attention away from a negative thought pattern, for example, towards something more positive, can re-wire your brain and increase its resilience.
- Insight alone does not produce lasting change but insight coupled with repeated practice does. Modalities like therapy and by extension coaching, reshape the brain in ways that show a reduction in amygdala activity and cerebral-based rumination and worry. The net effect is less anxiety and depression, along with greater self-regulation.
- The human brain finds uncertainty deeply unnerving because it interferes with the brain's prediction-making capabilities. While leaders can't always provide the certainty that their followers crave, providing clarity is a good substitute. Being transparent, eliminating some options, communicating how and when a decision will be made, and reiterating your guiding principles can go a long way toward calming an anxious system.
- Our nervous systems are "bound up with the nervous systems of other people." A leader's words and actions have a profound influence on what happens inside other people's bodies and brains, and other people have a similar effect on the leader. This process, known as co-regulation, has significant implications for how we engage with one another. Leaders who are mindful of this biological fact can create better listening in their followers, increase trust with others, and even reduce sickness, pain, and stress in the people they work and live with.

CHAPTER 11

PUTTING IT ALL TOGETHER
EMBODYING THE THREE RESILIENT LEADERSHIP IMPERATIVES

It is not the mountain we conquer, but ourselves

—Edmund Hillary

The movie *The King's Speech* tells the true story of King George VI as he worked to overcome his speech impediment and lead England through World War II with a historic speech. In one pivotal scene early in the movie, Prince George (about to become King George) meets for the first time with Lionel Logue, an Australian speech therapist. In his future role as King, George knows he will have to stand before his people and inspire them with his words. But he dreaded the prospect, knowing that he could barely string two sentences together without stammering and stuttering.

In his initial meeting with the speech therapist, Prince George is distant and curt. He makes it clear that he doesn't want to be there, and he desperately hopes for a quick fix. Throughout the conversation George stutters and stammers as he answers questions Lionel asks of him. His body posture is rigid and closed off, telegraphing his disdain for the situation in which he finds himself. At several points he struggles to contain his emotions and erupts in loud, angry outbursts.

In contrast, Lionel is composed, articulate and steady. He faces the King squarely, takes a deep breath and sits up tall to gather himself. While there is an obvious, enormous power difference between the two men (Lionel is a mere commoner and George is Royalty), it is clear that Lionel is not intimidated. Instead, he engages with the future king as an equal and from a place of strength. He is curious and inquisitive, seeking to better understand the man before him and what is at the root of his impediment. When the King challenges Lionel's thinking and expertise, he holds his ground with the Prince, calmly responding with statements like *"My castle my rules"* or *"It's my field and I can assure you no child starts talking with a stammer."*

In one particularly humorous exchange, Prince George lights up a cigarette and Lionel tells him not to do that, saying, *"I believe sucking smoke into your lungs will kill you."* While still holding the cigarette in his fingers, the prince replies, *"My physicians say smoking relaxes the throat,"* to which Lionel replies, *"They're idiots."* Prince George retorts, "They've all been knighted," and without missing a beat, Lionel dryly comments, *"That makes it official."*

Despite his initial skepticism, the King ends up hiring Lionel to help him overcome his speech impediment and the two men end up forging a life-long, enduring friendship based on mutual respect, shared values and genuine affection.

What's Going on Here?
In chapter 1 we introduced the three imperatives of a resilient leader: *Stay Calm, Stay the Course* and *Stay Connected.* We then devoted a separate chapter to each imperative, delving deeply into each one--what it is, how it works, and what leaders can do to develop that specific leadership capability. The true practice of resilient leadership, however, requires the ability to embody all three imperatives simultaneously--and in a balanced and fluid way. Lionel, in his very first meeting with the future King of England, was the quintessential example of what this looks like in action.

Let's take a closer look at how Lionel did just that:

Stay Calm: In the face of George's angry outbursts, Lionel does not allow himself to be triggered. Instead of reacting mindlessly to his provocation, Lionel centers himself and remains present, steady, calm and curious. This in turn lowers Prince George's anxiety. Lionel even uses playful humor to diffuse his anger.

Stay the Course: George seeks to undermine Lionel's expertise by suggesting that he does not know what he is talking about, and he tries to use his power and position to weaken Lionel's resolve. But Lionel is clear about the principles upon which his work is based and he refuses to waver from them. Instead, he is able to calmly yet firmly articulate his "house rules" and insist that George embrace them while they are together.

Stay Connected: In addition to being a calming presence and leading with conviction, Lionel is also able to stay *"close enough to influence, yet distant enough to lead."* He demonstrates empathy and genuine care for the future King, but not so much that he is willing to compromise on his principles. Even George's angry outbursts and childish behavior do not result in Lionel distancing from the King; rather, he stays emotionally present while remaining clear about his boundaries.

What makes Lionel's example such a helpful one is the way he demonstrated calm, conviction and connection, seamlessly and in just the right proportions, with neither imperative overshadowing the others. His calm demeanor was balanced by the clarity of his convictions and his willingness to give voice to them; and the clarity of his convictions was balanced by his equally powerful ability to stay connected – even to a highly reactive and anxious person who held power and position over him. This is the gold standard for leaders, and it is the work of a lifetime to seamlessly and consistently *stay calm, stay the course* and *stay connected* in all of our relationship systems, especially the ones that challenge us the most. When we do all three in a balanced and harmonious manner—especially in the face of reactivity and anxiety-driven sabotage—it makes all the difference.

The gold standard for leaders is to seamlessly and consistently stay calm, stay the course and stay connected in all of our relationship systems.

Stop & Reflect

- **Think about a challenging meeting or conversation that you handled particularly well, despite the anxiety and reactivity that was present (either in the other person, in you, or perhaps in both of you).**
- **As you reflect on this conversation, see if you can identify the specific ways that you embodied and communicated *staying calm, staying the course,* and *staying connected.* What resources did you draw upon to be present in this way?**

Striking a Balance

In our best moments, we are able to demonstrate the three imperatives in a balanced and fluid way, just as Lionel did with the future King of England. And yet, most leaders have greater strength in one or perhaps two of the imperatives. Rarely is a leader naturally gifted in equal measure across all three. This is exactly why, if leaders are not mindful and intentional, they can end up expressing themselves in an unbalanced fashion, falling short of their potential to lead others in transformative ways. Like muscles in the body, when one area gets overworked, others can weaken and atrophy in ways that make a leader less effective.

For example, imagine a leader who is particularly strong in staying the course. This leader has no hesitation about taking tough stands, speaking her mind and being clear about what she expects from others. She can command a room and be passionately inspiring. This is a great strength, yet this leader has utilized and relied upon this strength far more often than she has focused on *staying calm* and *staying connected*. As a result, when she speaks with conviction (particularly when she is disappointed or upset), it often comes at the cost of staying emotionally present to the people she is leading. Her default under pressure is to withdraw. And her strong stands can be spoken from a reactive and rigid place. When this is the case, her message is not heard nearly as well as it could have been, had she embodied a calmer presence and stayed more mindfully connected.

Now imagine another leader who is particularly strong in *staying connected*. This leader has an uncanny ability to read others, is highly empathetic and cares deeply about the people he leads. His ability to forge healthy, trusting relationships with colleagues and direct reports is a great strength. Yet this strength exceeds his ability to stay calm and to stay the course. During times of heightened stress and uncertainty, he often fails to regulate his own anxiety and has difficulty taking tough, unpopular stands. Under pressure he will not lose connection, but he sometimes loses his voice. As a result, he is seen as a trusted leader, but not a particularly powerful or influential one.

Lastly, imagine a leader whose greatest strength is *staying calm* – being thoughtful and non-reactive under pressure. This leader is consistently calm not only when navigating the day-to-day pressures of her job but also in the big moments, during times of crisis or disruptive change. Her steadiness at the wheel engenders confidence and helps others to lessen their own anxiety when the winds of change blow. Her ability to stay calm is clearly a great strength, yet it sometimes overshadows her ability to speak assertively, especially during heated or tense conversations. As a result, she is viewed as a calm

Leaders who practiced bringing a balanced measure of staying calm, staying the course, and staying connected expanded their credibility and positive impact on others.

leader, but sometimes to a fault. In certain situations, when she stays quiet instead of speaking up with conviction, some people interpret her calm demeanor as a lack of passion, energy or engagement.

These three examples represent leaders that Bridgette and Bob have worked with over the years, each of whom grew to become better differentiated by intentionally working on and strengthening the under-developed "muscles" in their leadership repertoire. As they practiced bringing a balanced measure of staying calm, staying the course, and staying connected, their credibility as leaders expanded as did their positive impact on others.

Stop & Reflect

- **How would you assess your current ability to embody all three imperatives in a balanced and fluid way?**
- **Which of the three imperatives is your greatest strength? Which one do you find most challenging to embody on a consistent basis?**

Maria's Story

It's no secret that healthcare workers bore the brunt of the pandemic as they cared for the sick, while their own safety and the safety of their families were at risk. Many healthcare leaders stepped forward to provide the calm, steady, and courageous leadership that was needed during that perilous time. Bridgette was privileged to work with one of these leaders during the pandemic – a hospital administrator named Maria. She was the CEO of one of the biggest hospitals in Boston during the pandemic, and her job was to lead the hospital while also being the public face of the hospital to the outside world.

During one of their early coaching sessions, Maria shared with Bridgette that she had been approached by a larger hospital to interview for a more senior job – one that in fact was two levels above her current position. Maria had not sought out this opportunity and was in fact surprised that she was being considered. It was going to be a challenging role that involved merging several hospitals into one system and there would be no shortage of pitfalls and problems awaiting whomever took on the role.

"I'm not certain I'm cut out for this role," Maria confided to Bridgette, and then she added, "and I frankly don't know why they've sought me out when there are other administrators with bigger resumes than mine."

Before Maria had started working with Bridgette, she had already led the hospital through the most turbulent phase of the pandemic. Bridgette asked Maria to share with her how she had led during that time. What became clear as Maria shared her experience is that she had embodied a masterful blend of staying calm, staying the course and staying connected. Her well-differentiated leadership had not only steadied an anxious organization, it had also caught the eye of senior leaders in the hospital system.

What's Going on Here?

Like many leaders, Maria was unconsciously competent regarding several of her strengths. She led brilliantly by deploying her instincts and intuition during a once-in-a-lifetime global pandemic, but she didn't know or couldn't see why she had been so successful. By identifying the value and impact of her ability to stay calm, stay the course and stay connected, Maria came to understand why she was being sought after for a visible and highly competitive position. Like Lionel the speech therapist, Maria's "secret sauce" was her seamless and balanced embodiment of the three imperatives of resilient leaders. Now that she had the language to describe her strengths, Maria was poised to leverage them more intentionally. RL's 3 imperatives are always needed to calm the regressive and dysfunctional patterns of anxious organizations; but in the VUCA world we live in today, it is the "secret sauce" that sets resilient leaders apart.

Implementing the right mix of the three imperatives is the "secret sauce" of resilient leaders.

The Taste Test

Carrying this metaphor a bit further, imagine you were mixing ingredients into a bowl to make a special sauce for dinner guests. At some point in the process, you would likely do a taste test to see if you needed to add a pinch more of one ingredient or another. Based on your assessment, you might adjust the composition of the sauce before serving it to make sure you got it just right.

Similarly, you can check the strength and consistency of these three ingredients in your own leadership practice. A good question to ask yourself is this: *What is going on within me and around me at this moment in time? In light of this, which of the three resilient leadership imperatives does my team or organization need more of from me?*

Suppose you have been distracted and distant at work and more absent than usual due to competing priorities and stressors on the home front. If so, perhaps a pinch more of Staying Connected is needed. Do you find yourself feeling tense and overly reactive to the triggers in your day? Then perhaps a deliberate focus on Staying Calm, and in particular calming your nervous system, is the best thing you could do for your team right now. Or maybe there is an unresolved issue at work that you've been avoiding. Facing it square on may require a stronger dose of conviction and an ability to Stay the Course in the face of resistance and pushback.

Once you know which ingredient may be a bit lacking, the right question to ask yourself is: *What's a good next step I could take to bring more of this ingredient to the mix?*

Embodying the Three Imperatives

Martha Graham, one of the most celebrated dancers of the 20th century, recounts her life's work in her autobiography titled, *Blood Memory*. In the book she tells the story of her father catching her in a lie when she was a young girl. When she asked him how he knew she wasn't telling the truth, he replied simply, "The body never lies."

This quote is a powerful reminder of the important role our body plays in communicating trust and credibility. A leader's body language telegraphs volumes of information to those around him about his inner state – his deeper emotions, moods and intentions. Some of these underlying emotions may not be consciously known or recognized by the leader, but they show up in their body nevertheless.

A leader might claim he is calm, but if his body is tense, his jaw clenched and his brows furrowed, no one will believe his claim. If a leader communicates to his team his expectations and tells them he will hold them accountable, but does so with a slightly collapsed spine and shoulders curved inward, others will see equivocation rather than resolve. And if a leader says he is open to new ideas, but communicates this message with his arms crossed tightly over his chest and eyes narrowed, he will likely communicate a closed state of mind rather than an open one.

The bottom line? If there is any hint of disparity between a leader's words and his body language, people will trust what the leader's body is saying over his words. If you want to be a leader who consistently stays calm, stays the course and stays connected, you will need to practice these imperatives until they become embedded in your body and expressed in your posture, facial expressions, and the way you sit, stand and walk through your day.

A leader's body language telegraphs volumes of information to those around him about his inner state – his deeper emotions, moods and intentions.

Embodiment means moving beyond intellectual understanding where we grasp something with our minds, to understanding something at a deeper level, where we can express it with our whole body and way of being. This requires consistent, steady practice over time that involves not just our thinking self, but our physical self as well.

Two of the practices we've included in this book, 6-second Centering and Embody Your Length, are aimed directly at helping you to do just that. On the next page we offer one additional practice for building greater muscle memory and embodiment of resilient leadership.

Core Practice

Embodying the Three "Stays"

The following practice can be done at the beginning of your day, at the end of it, or anytime you want to center yourself in the three imperatives of a resilient leader.

Sit comfortably in a chair and take a deep, mindful breath. Breathe in for the count of five and exhale for the count of five a few times, until you begin to feel present.

Stay Calm: Aim the spotlight of your attention on your body. Notice your jaw, your shoulders, your neck, and your upper back. If you detect tension in any of these areas, relax them. Pay particular attention to your shoulders, which often rise up towards the ears when we are anxious. Continue to inhale deeply and fully, allowing your chest to rise and fall naturally with the breath. Notice the calm you are feeling as you attend to your body and release the anxious tension it holds.

Stay the Course: Now put both feet flat on the floor and sit up tall. Recall something in your leadership or life that you are deeply committed to. Consider the values you hold near and dear and the things you genuinely stand for. Use this moment to connect with the guiding principles you aspire to lead and live by. Is it courage? Integrity? Loyalty? Notice the resolve that arises as you reconnect with the values and convictions that give you energy and life.

Stay Connected: With your body calm and your convictions in clear view, aim your attention towards someone you genuinely care about, whether a colleague, a friend, or a family member. Picture this person in your mind's eye and see them as if they are standing in front of you. Holding this image in your imagination, take another deep, mindful breath, filling your chest and allowing the muscles there to stretch and open. Take your right hand and place it over your heart. This gesture is meant to soften the heart, which we often keep protected and guarded during times of stress and strain. Notice the connection you feel when you allow your chest and heart to open in the presence of someone you care about.

Chapter Summary

- The "secret sauce" of resilient leaders is the ability to stay calm, stay the course and stay connected in a balanced and fluid way, even in the midst of anxious others. It is this capacity that differentiates resilient leaders and sets them apart from the crowd.
- Most leaders are more naturally gifted in one of the three imperatives, sometimes to the detriment of the others. Knowing which one is your greatest strength, and then mindfully building strength in the others, will help you to become a more credible and influential leader.
- A leader's body language telegraphs volumes of information about their inner state – their emotions, moods and frame of mind. The leader may not be conscious of these deeper emotions, but they show up in the body nevertheless.
- If there is any daylight between what a leader says and what their body language telegraphs, people will believe the latter over the former.
- Embodiment means grasping something not just at an intellectual level, but at a muscular level. It requires steady practice over time that involves not just our thinking self but our physical self as well.

CONCLUSION to the First Edition

RESILIENT LEADERS BUILD RESILIENT ORGANIZATIONS

A fundamental tenet of all of the training and coaching that we do is our frequent admonition that the primary responsibility of those who wish to become resilient leaders is to focus first and foremost on their own functioning. In each chapter of this book, the Three Big Ideas offer leaders practical steps they can take to develop their own capacity...

> to lead with calm, clarity, and conviction in the midst of anxiety provoked by increasing complexity and accelerating change—to lead from strength, and know how to care for themselves emotionally, spiritually, and physically and sustain their leadership efforts over time.

While our primary focus has been on the person of the leader, the subtext has always been about the benefit that accrues to the organization(s) the leader is a part of. Our understanding of how systems work has convinced us that even a single person who practices Resilient Leadership—regardless of what position that person may occupy in the organization—can promote healthier functioning in the overall system. Naturally, an individual at the top of the system will have more leverage and a broader opportunity to influence the organization at large, but even at a level well below the C-suite, the person who shows up as a resilient leader can be confident that s/he is making a significant contribution to the positive functioning of the entire system.

Resilient Organizations

Our experience has also shown us that the more individuals there are in an organization who learn about and practice Resilient Leadership, the quicker and better will the system reflect the qualities we associate with a Resilient Organization. We call your attention to the Appendix (page 242), where we have provided a quick set of survey questions to help you assess "How Resilient Is Your Team?" As you read through those questions, you will see how they contribute to our description of Resilient Organizations as those that **have the leadership capability they need to face and surmount in a sustainable way adaptive challenges (i.e., those for which there are currently no existing solutions within the organization).** Such organizations are characterized by a high degree of organizational health.

Organizational Health

The notion of organizational health is something that Patrick Lencioni has picked up on in his book *The Advantage*, where he distinguishes between "smart" organizations and "healthy" organizations. The characteristics of what he calls smart organizations fit into what we describe as the rational system of an organization, while the signs he sees of a healthy organization (minimal politics, minimal confusion, high morale, high productivity, low turnover) are some of the benefits we have seen result from organizations where resilient leaders pay attention to the emotional system. We also agree with Lencioni's assertion that although both are essential for success, healthy is more important than smart and "trumps everything else in business." Our way of saying this is: without a healthy balance in the emotional system, even the best rational system will not be able to function at peak performance. The core thesis of this book is that a leader who operates out of the Resilient Leadership perspective with a New

Way of SEEING, THINKING, and LEADING holds the key to developing a Resilient Organization.

Take the Next Steps

If you have found the message of this book persuasive—or even intriguing enough to investigate further—we encourage you to take the next step toward becoming a more resilient leader by putting in place a plan of action. When we offer Resilient Leadership training, we encourage participants to create a Personal Development Plan in which they identify their areas of strength and their growth areas as well as what Resilient Leadership competencies they wish to cultivate. Then, using a coach, a peer group, a mentor, or some other support structure (this is not work you can do alone!), they are encouraged to set in place specific goals that begin a lifelong journey of growth.

The goals need to be SMART ("specific, measurable, achievable, results-focused, and time-bound"), and, in whatever way works best, there needs to be some accountability structure that will both challenge and support the leaders to ensure that the progress they make is sustainable.

We also encourage participants in our programs to pick one or two of the Resilient Leadership Core Practices to incorporate into their routine on a daily or weekly basis, because insight alone is not enough to produce meaningful behavior change. Becoming a more resilient leader takes consistent, sustained practice, just like any other arena of development. We invite you to do the same by reviewing the list of Core Practices included in our Appendix (page 255) and selecting one or two that you commit to using regularly. You might also wish to review the list of questions we've captured in the Appendix (page 249) to see if there are any you might want to ask yourself (or your team) on a recurring basis to promote a New Way of SEEING, THINKING, or LEADING.

A Lifelong Process

Many experts in Bowen Theory and Resilient Leadership—Bridgette and Bob included—have made the personal discovery that growth in self-differentiation nearly always requires supportive structures to foster and focus our efforts. So much of what is called for in the exercise of Resilient Leadership is counterintuitive, or—perhaps better said—involves going beyond our instinctive, automatic functioning. Roberta Gilbert served on the faculty of the Bowen Center for many years. In her book *Extraordinary Leadership*, she says:

> Learning to think systems…is a continuing process and a lot of work on self in one's systems. As far as I can tell, those of us who are serious about thinking systems, need to stay in touch with others thinking systems…the rest of our lives. I do. I meet with colleagues on a regular basis in order to keep my head thinking systems and out of "cause and effect" thinking, blame, and individual thinking. *All of us revert to these modes unless there is a special effort to prevent ourselves from turning back to more automatic ways of thinking* (page 182).

Unless we are reminded regularly to be deliberate about our practice of Resilient Leadership, we all too easily revert to inherited patterns that may or may not best serve our own growth and the healthy functioning of the systems we lead. Should you wish to explore further opportunities for yourself or your organization to embrace Resilient Leadership as a way of being, we encourage you to contact us via our website www.ResilientLeadershipDevelopment.com. You will also find there a template for a Personal Development Plan that we encourage you to use to guide and focus the steps you will take to become a more resilient leader.

CONCLUSION to the Second Edition

As we were writing the opening pages of Chapter 1 in the First Edition of this book, we invoked the notion of a "paradigm shift" to describe our conviction that the Resilient Leadership model brings something truly new to the understanding and practice of leadership. Now, as we conclude work on the revision and expansion of this volume nearly a decade later, we are more confident than ever that the Resilient Leadership model offers unique insights, encourages powerful behaviors, and provides fresh perspectives on leadership.

Time and time again, we have been privileged to witness both aspiring and seasoned leaders discover what these phrases mean: "Stay Calm", "Stay Connected", and "Stay the Course". We have seen that the growth and the changes are gradual and incremental at first, but that the results can be transformational—both for the individual leader and for the systems they are part of.

New behaviors that begin tentatively grow into skills that are tested and strong; insights that start out as curious questions accumulate and gather momentum as "Ah-Ha" moments multiply. Sometimes the changes are felt first at home—where they can be tested with trusted partners; for others the workplace becomes a learning organization—where colleagues start to share the RL jargon of "triangles" and "reactivity" and "overfunctioning" until "a new way of seeing" and "systems thinking" gradually replace linear thinking and a focus on the rational system alone.

Updating *Resilient Leadership 2.0* has been rewarding for us as we've gathered new content and materials from the training and coaching that the Resilient Leadership LLC team has done in recent years. We have continued to deepen our understanding of our "source code" as we have been constantly challenged to find new and better ways to help you apply fresh RL insights to your lives at home and at work, in ways large and small.

For all our stakeholders who have shared this journey with us, we are grateful. As we look forward to the benefits still to be realized from the practice of Resilient Leadership, we are convinced that **the best is yet to come!**

Bob Duggan & Bridgette Theurer

APPENDIX to the First Edition

Are You a Step-Down Transformer?

A *step-down transformer* is a leader who exerts a calming influence not only in acute situations but also in the midst of routine, daily pressures and stressors. To assess the extent to which you currently operate as a step-down transformer for your team, rate yourself on the following scale: 0 = rarely true, 1 = sometimes true, 2 = often true. Use your results to pinpoint areas of strength and areas you can improve with intentional practice.

_____ When I walk into a room where tensions and emotions are running high, my presence tends to have a calming effect on others and promotes greater thoughtfulness.

_____ If there is confusion on my team about roles, responsibilities, or priorities, I step in quickly to provide clarity and direction.

_____ I notice when people are making untested assumptions, passing judgments, or gossiping, and I refocus them on the facts.

_____ When others want a quick fix, I become curious and ask questions rather than simply react.

_____ When the mood on my team becomes deadly serious, I use playfulness and/or humor to lighten things up and to defuse tensions.

_____ I don't take myself too seriously.

_____ I notice when I am feeling and/or telegraphing anxiety and take steps to lower it so that I don't "infect" others.

_____ When I notice that members of my team are becoming reactive, rather than pass judgment, I get curious about what might be going on in the system (or in them) and take steps calculated to lower anxiety.

_____ I take responsibility for my own reactive behaviors and engage in daily/weekly practices (e.g., exercise, yoga, meditation, centering, etc.) that help me to lower my anxiety and stay calm under pressure.

_____

Total

Results:
0-10: Lots of growth potential. Challenge yourself to do better.
11-15: Quite acceptable. But still room for improvement.
16-18: Very impressive. Are you really that good?

Reactive Behaviors Inventory

To be a Less Anxious Presence requires that we become more astute observers of our own brand of reactivity—those behaviors we exhibit automatically when we are anxious or under pressure—and then learn ways to manage ourselves so that these behaviors lessen over time. Check off those behaviors below that you see in yourself when you feel threatened or stressed. You may want to ask a trusted colleague or family member to complete this inventory for you as well, since all of us can be blind to our own reactivity.

______ Excessive worrying

______ Walking and talking fast or frenetically

______ Interrupting others in conversation

______ Distancing from others

______ Engaging in combative behaviors

______ Avoiding or suppressing conflict

______ Finding fault and blaming others

______ Being controlling of outcomes, projects, or people

______ Pushing ourselves or others too hard

______ Micromanaging

______ Complaining about a colleague to others (triangulating)

______ Shutting down emotionally

______ Seeking a quick fix

______ Failing to be direct and decisive when needed

______ Giving up our voice or resigning in place

______ Being overly analytical and missing the bigger picture

______ Being too quick to rescue others who are struggling

______ Drinking excessively or eating poorly

How Resilient is Your Team?

Resilient teams have the leadership capability they need to face and surmount adaptive challenges sustainably. They are also characterized by a high degree of collaboration, creative thinking, mutual support and challenge, shared goals and core principles. Think about one of the teams that you belong to and indicate how frequently the following statements apply:

0 = Never   1= Occasionally   2 = Frequently   3 = Nearly Always

In my team...

_____ a sense of urgency can be brought to bear on important issues and challenges, without stirring up high levels of anxiety and reactivity in the process.

_____ team members are engaged and commitment is high.

_____ innovation, creativity and thoughtful risk-taking are encouraged and visible.

_____ the team is cohesive and characterized by high levels of trust.

_____ communication within the team is strong and healthy.

_____ when a breakdown occurs, cool heads typically prevail because members are thoughtful and non-anxious.

_____ clarity and shared understanding around purpose, priorities and direction is cultivated and reinforced.

_____ members know how to manage their capacity so that they can reliably satisfy stakeholder needs, without burning themselves (or others) out.

_____ a sense of realistic optimism about meeting goals and achieving success permeates.

_____ members hold one another accountable for their commitments and performance in a timely and respectful way

_____ individuals who take a clear stand based on conviction or principle are met with respect, even by those who might

see things differently.
_____ we discourage reactive behaviors such as gossiping, rumor-mongering, blaming, scapegoating, and mindless "group-think".
_____ there is relatively little turnover due to conflict within the group
_____ we are regarded positively by other groups or teams within the organization
_____ when the landscape changes, we respond by making timely and thoughtful changes to address the new realities.

_____
Total

Results:
0-20: Your team has low levels of resilience
21-35: Your team has moderate levels of resilience
36-45: Your team has high levels of resilience

Poorly Differentiated Leadership vs. Well-Differentiated Leadership

A Poorly Differentiated Leader:
Focuses on weaknesses (her/his own and others)
Works with symptomatic people
Seeks relief of symptoms (rather than causes)
"Betters" the condition
Is concerned to give insight
Just tries harder when a problem recurs
Diagnoses others
Is quick to quit difficult situations
Is made anxious by reactivity
Sees a problem as a cause of anxiety
Adapts to the weak
Has an empathic focus on helpless victims
Is more likely to create dependent relationships
Avoids conflict

A Well-Differentiated Leader:
Focuses on strengths (her/his own and others)
Works with motivated people
Matures the system
Seeks enduring change
Is concerned to define self (take stands)
Is fed up with a recurrent problem and reframes the issue
Analyzes his/her own stuckness
Sees difficult situations as stimulating challenges
Recognizes that reactivity (sabotage) is a natural response to a system that is being challenged
Sees a problem as a symptom of anxiety
Adapts toward strengths
Takes a challenging attitude that encourages responsibility for self
Is more likely to create balanced relationships
Faces and resolves conflict

Are You a Systems Thinker?

Leaders "think systems" by reflecting thoughtfully on the actions, reactions, and interactions they have observed among the people within the emotional system of which they are a part. In thinking systems, a leader seeks to understand more deeply how these interactions form patterns that may be hindering (or promoting) effective action. To assess the extent to which you currently *think systems,* rate yourself on the following scale: 0 = rarely true; 1 = sometimes true; 2 = often true. Use your results to pinpoint areas of strength and areas you can improve with intentional practice.

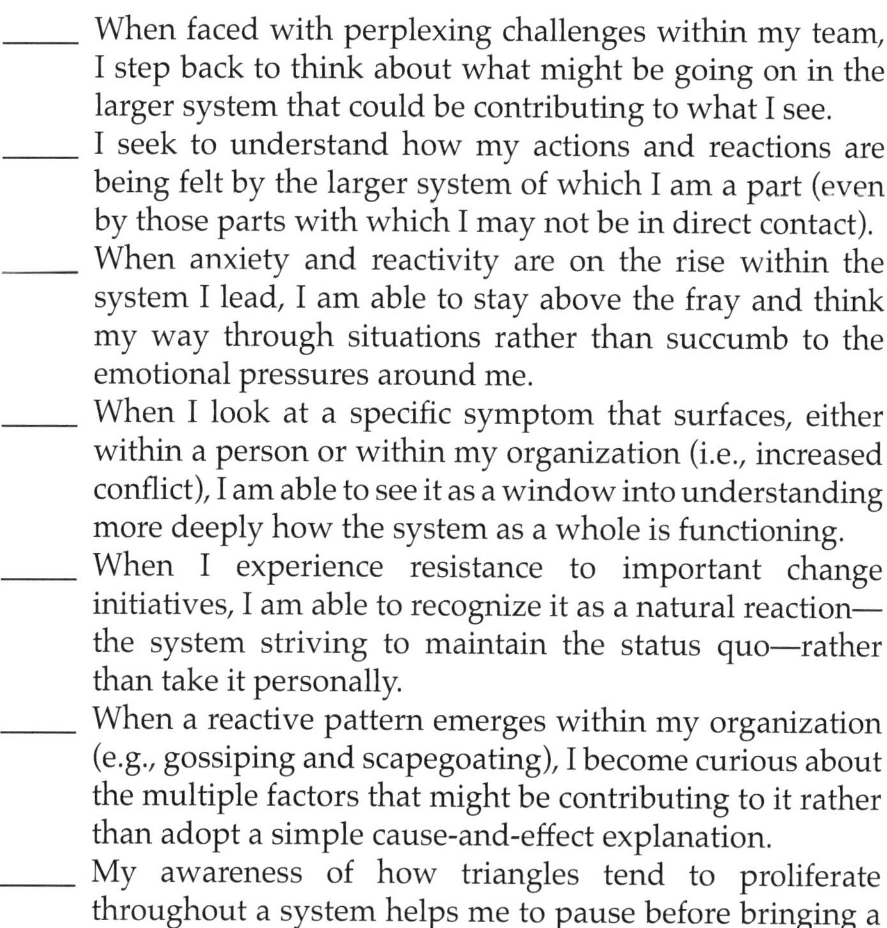

_____ When faced with perplexing challenges within my team, I step back to think about what might be going on in the larger system that could be contributing to what I see.

_____ I seek to understand how my actions and reactions are being felt by the larger system of which I am a part (even by those parts with which I may not be in direct contact).

_____ When anxiety and reactivity are on the rise within the system I lead, I am able to stay above the fray and think my way through situations rather than succumb to the emotional pressures around me.

_____ When I look at a specific symptom that surfaces, either within a person or within my organization (i.e., increased conflict), I am able to see it as a window into understanding more deeply how the system as a whole is functioning.

_____ When I experience resistance to important change initiatives, I am able to recognize it as a natural reaction—the system striving to maintain the status quo—rather than take it personally.

_____ When a reactive pattern emerges within my organization (e.g., gossiping and scapegoating), I become curious about the multiple factors that might be contributing to it rather than adopt a simple cause-and-effect explanation.

_____ My awareness of how triangles tend to proliferate throughout a system helps me to pause before bringing a third party into an anxious situation between myself and another person.

_____ When people try to involve me in their issues with another person or department, I am able to maintain emotional neutrality and avoid taking sides.

_____ When I am not getting the results I want from my team, one of the first questions I ask myself is, "What's my part in this?"

_____
Total

Results:
0-10: Lots of growth potential. Challenge yourself to do better.
11-15: Quite acceptable. But still room for improvement.
16-18: Very impressive. Are you really that good?

Sources of Chronic Anxiety

Chronic anxiety is an abiding state of unease that lies just beneath our conscious awareness. Managing or reducing it is an essential part of becoming a more resilient leader. Yet given that chronic anxiety is beneath our conscious awareness, how can we do this? Described below are some of the sources of chronic anxiety. They can shed light on what contributes to this abiding state of unease and provide clues to how we might manage it better.

Human beings crave some measure of **control, safety, approval, belonging,** and **certainty** to feel secure in the world. When we perceive that one or more of these primal needs are being threatened, our level of chronic anxiety increases, giving rise to more reactive behaviors. While all of these needs are important, usually one or two are particularly potent sources of anxiety for us. Which of these is most triggering for you?

Control: When we sense we are losing control, our instinctive response is to reassert ourselves to regain control. Our need for autonomy may make us overfunction, micromanage, or indulge in other behaviors that we feel will lower anxiety. However, reactive behaviors only perpetuate and can even increase our level of chronic anxiety rather than make us more calm and thoughtful. What are some more thoughtful responses that help you lower anxiety when you are feeling threatened with a loss of control?

Safety: All of us possess a deep-seated need to feel both physically and emotionally safe. When we feel a heightened vulnerability to threats, our immediate instinct is to adopt one of the classic automatic responses—fight or flight, freeze or appease, or tend and befriend. These instinctual, reflex behaviors can express themselves in many different ways. How do they most often show up among your repertoire of responses, either at work or at home?

Approval: We are by nature social beings, and receiving messages of approval from significant others is an essential ingredient in the formation of a healthy self-concept. When we lack a sufficient level of approval in childhood or even into adulthood, we can begin to question our self-worth. That insecurity can erode our ability to function in a strong and healthy way and often leads to defensive posturing or inauthentic ways of showing up in relationships. Do your approval needs ever get in the way of taking a strong and clear stand on issues? How do you find within yourself the resources to lower anxiety in this area so that you can more easily choose an unpopular path and hold firm, even when your decision encounters opposition?

Belonging: Being part of a tribe is an important component of our identity, and affiliation needs drive many of our behaviors on an unconscious level. Leaders who recognize the power of our need to belong can use this insight to build a strong team spirit among workplace associates, multiplying their effectiveness many times over. A strong, felt sense of belonging lowers anxiety. What techniques to lower anxiety have you found most helpful in motivating others, building coalitions, and winning over those who resist change?

Certainty: All of us crave certainty because it gives us a greater sense of security and control. But in today's workplace, even in the best of circumstances, uncertainty is more often the norm rather than the exception. Becoming more comfortable with the presence of uncertainty allows us to be prudent risk-takers instead of playing catch-up as late adopters of new ideas, technology, and the like. What most helps you to lower your anxiety in the face of uncertainty so that you can be a more thoughtful risk-taker and innovator?

Questions to Ask Yourself or Those You Lead/Coach/Mentor

Be a Step-Down Transformer

- When was the last time you were able to exert a calming influence on an anxious or tense situation? What did you do to lower anxiety and promote greater thoughtfulness?
- What makes you anxious, and how does anxiety show up in your body and behavior?
- What triggers your reactivity (people, events, issues, etc.)?
- What practices or habits help you to manage your reactivity/calm down?
- What behaviors best alert you that anxiety is escalating in your team/organization?
- What projects, relationships, or initiatives could benefit from a more calm, clear, and consistent presence from you? What might this look like in action?

Stay Connected

- To what extent have you been emotionally present and available to the system(s) that you lead in the last week? In the last month?
- As a leader, what is your default tendency under pressure and stress—to distance yourself from others or to become too close with them?
- Which people at work might you be too close to or even fused with? Which people at work might you be too distant from?
- How well do you balance stepping in to give guidance and support and stepping out to let others do their jobs?
- What might you need to do more of as a leader right now—to stand apart from or to stand with others? What might this look like?
- What is the one thing you could do that would have the biggest impact on improving the quality of your connection with those you lead?

Lead with Conviction

- Describe a time when you led boldly and with conviction. What did you do? What were you standing for?
- How do you typically react to resistance? What forms of resistance trigger you the most?
- What are the guiding principles or values that you live and lead by? Why are these important to you?
- Are there specific places in your leadership or life where you see a need for greater boldness on your part? What might that look like?
- What projects, issues, or situations need a clearer stand from you?
- What is your vision of the future for your team/organization? To what extent is there shared understanding of it among those you lead?

Balance the Seesaw (Over/Underfunctioning)

- What triggers you to overfunction as a leader?
- To what extent are overfunctioners rewarded in your organization?
- Are any of your direct reports over- or underfunctioning right now? If so, what is the impact on them? On others?
- If you are a parent with children in the home, are you overfunctioning for them in any way? If so, what is the impact on you? On them?
- Which departments or teams within your organization consistently overfunction, and which ones consistently underfunction? What steps might you take to help correct this pattern?
- What are the biggest stumbling blocks you might encounter in your efforts to stop the over/underfunctioning cycle that you are engaged in? What risks are involved?

Manage Triangles

- How easy or challenging is it for you to maintain emotional neutrality when you are in an anxious triangle with the important people in your life?
- Are there any other relationships with significant people in your life that you feel responsible for fixing? How does your anxiety manifest itself in your behavior?
- When an employee or colleague comes to you to complain or vent about another colleague, how do you typically respond? Does your response raise or lower the reactivity in your system?
- Consider an anxious triangle you are part of on the home front. How might you show up in that triangle in a less anxious way?
- Consider an anxious triangle you are part of on the work front. How might you show up in that triangle in a less anxious way?
- Are there specific people or departments in your organization that chronically form toxic triangles? How might you be a calming, less reactive influence on them?

Generation to Generation

- What strengths did you inherit from your family of origin, and how have they shaped you as a leader?
- Do you think you inherited any vulnerabilities or weaknesses from your family of origin and if so, how do they impact you as a leader (a tendency to overfunction, for example)?
- What inherited patterns from the emotional system of your organization continue to exert a toxic influence on you or others (e.g., a tendency to tolerate poor performers)? What reactive behaviors surface as a result?
- Where is it easier for you to recognize the influence of these patterns—at work or at home? Where is it more difficult for you to manage the influence that inherited patterns exert on you—at work or at home?
- Who in your immediate or extended family might help you most to explore and understand the inherited strengths and vulnerabilities of your family system? How might you approach these relatives to help you do "research" that will deepen your understanding of your family inheritance?

- Who at work can help you explore the legacy of previous generations, especially reactive relationship patterns that continue to surface during anxious times?

Avoid the Empathy Trap

- What is easier and more natural for you to do—to offer comfort to those who are struggling or to challenge them to rise up and persevere?
- Can you think of a time when you (or someone you know) stepped in too quickly to rescue someone from a challenging situation? What was the impact of that rescuing behavior?
- How well do you as a leader set clear boundaries for those in your organization who may be poorly differentiated and invasive of others?
- To what extent can you tolerate the discomfort or pain of others as they are working their way through a challenging situation? To the extent that it is needed, how can you grow your own tolerance for the pain of others?
- In your organization, do poor performers tend to be rescued or overly empathized with, or appropriately challenged? What is the impact on people? What is the impact on results?

Promoting a Sense of Urgency vs. Raising Anxiety

A Thoughtful Response to Perceived Threats: Promoting Urgency and Innovation

- Recognize that you are anxious and be curious about what is causing it.
- Get on the balcony to observe what is going on and your role in it.
- Lower your stress response through centering, breathing, taking a walk, etc., *so you can think more clearly.*
- Step back and assess the perceived threat, how real it is, and what you and your team can do about it.
- Focus on the facts—what you know and what is not known—rather than making untested assumptions or speculating about causes, motives, etc.
- Communicate as transparently and as clearly as possible about the nature of the perceived threat, the resources available to respond, and the givens (boundaries) within which you can operate.
- Speak with grounded optimism: be open and candid about the real threats and challenges your team/organization faces, why you are still hopeful about the future in spite of them, and the game plan for addressing them.
- Get perspective by involving an objective outsider to help you reframe or refocus the issue.
- Answer the questions, "What will likely happen if I/we do nothing?" and, "What is possible if we take effective action?" Share your thinking about this with those who must act.
- Take action based on your best thinking (and the best thinking of your team).

A Reactive Response to Perceived Threats: Escalating Anxiety

- Form a triangle to vent and to disperse your anxiety.
- Take action from an anxious place before calming yourself down so you can think more clearly.
- Assume the perceived threat is as real and as big as it feels (without testing out your assumptions to assess if they are valid or accurate).
- Look for a quick fix versus considering a range of options.
- Take actions that make you feel better but that actually perpetuate your anxiety in the long run: drinking, skipping meals, not sleeping, pushing yourself and others harder, etc.
- Fall back into your habitual ways of behaving when anxious (micromanaging, hiding out in your office, cutting off from others, blaming and scapegoating, stirring up conflict or avoiding it altogether, etc.).

Resilient Leadership Core Practices

Resilient Leadership
- Get On the Balcony
- Focus On Your Own Functioning

Be a Step-Down Transformer
- Six-Second Centering
- Cultivate a Curious Mind-Set

Lead with Conviction
- Communicate Where You Stand
- Embody Your Length

Stay Connected
- Be Separate yet Stay Connected
- E-Mail Mindfully

Balance the Seesaw
- Balance the Seesaw

Manage Triangles
- Hit the Pause Button before Triangulating
- Practice Emotional Neutrality

Generation to Generation
- Observe Your Inherited Vulnerabilities
- Observe Your Inherited Strengths

Avoid the Empathy Trap
- Ask What Is Most Needed
- Pause Before Rescuing or Distancing

APPENDIX
to the Second Edition

How to Tame Your Triggers

In our chapter on neuroscience (and in several other places in this volume), we have referred to the fact that all of us carry within ourselves a very significant (and idiosyncratic) list of stimuli (people, situations, etc.) that trigger in us automatic, reactive responses. These responses involve dimensions that are neurochemical, emotional, psychological, cognitive, and attitudinal—to mention just a few—and that result in a variety of behavioral manifestations, both positive and negative.

The very good news that is foundational to all Resilient Leadership's training and coaching efforts is that with sustained focus and persistent effort, each of us can become a better-differentiated leader. Emerging studies of neuroplasticity have shown that when an individual is sufficiently motivated and is in touch with the right resources and has a robust support system, it is both possible and likely that they can re-wire their brain and develop more appropriate and more effective leadership competencies and behaviors.

Below is a simple, accessible structure that will support you in your efforts to tame your reactive triggers and build a stronger, more mature repertoire of responses to your problematic triggers and their undesirable responses.

STEP ONE: Identify Your Triggers

- Look at the checklist of triggers on page 261 and reflect on which ones have caused you to behave in ways you now know could have (and should have) been better. Reflect quietly and thoughtfully on the people and situations that have often provoked your more regrettable feelings, thoughts, and actions.
- Name the triggers you are most susceptible to.

STEP TWO: Reflect on Your Automatic Reactions

- With a curious mindset, observe in a detached but interested way how your triggers in the past have operated "automatically" within you. This means that your reactions to the triggers were spontaneous and without forethought. For example did you become combative when triggered, or did you shut down? Did you become defensive or point a finger at the other person? Perhaps you "went along to get along" but quietly resented doing so. Every person has their own unique way of reacting to triggering events. Just observe without judgement and stick with your observations until they become quite granular and detailed. Notice in particular the impact your automatic reactions had on you, the other people involved and the quality of your connection with them.
- Capture any insights your observations have resulted in. It is particularly valuable when you can see connections and the resulting patterns that emerge.

STEP THREE: Observe in Real Time

- Steps One and Two will have heightened your awareness and given you a more nuanced ability to see in real-time how the stimulus-response dynamic plays out in you around the people and situations that make up your unique blend of triggers. Commit yourself to monitoring and tracking this dynamic for a specific timeframe. You may want to focus on only one trigger, or more than one. We suggest two weeks as a manageable period but choose a timeframe that you can realistically commit to. Set up your own chart to record the details that you find most helpful to note, recording your observations of the familiar pattern(s) you've come to recognize in Steps One and Two.

STEP FOUR: Interrupt the Pattern(s)

- Your focused attention and your deliberate intention to be less reactive to one or more triggers will gradually result in an enhanced ability to be more thoughtful, and less reactive. You will find the time between the "automatic" trigger and your awareness of being triggered is shrinking, which will allow you to manage your reactivity more quickly.
- Keep a log of your successes in which you note what helped you get more quickly "on the balcony", and what steps you took so that you "have" the trigger, rather than the trigger "having" you. Observe what works best to help you become less driven by your problematic trigger(s). It may be a quiet pause or a deep breath or two, or mentally repeating a favorite calming mantra, or something else. Keep practicing until you sense the new pattern is becoming as automatic as the old pattern.

STEP FIVE: Distil Your Practice into a Winning Formula

- Remember what we know about neuroplasticity and how much repetitive practice is required to lay down new neural pathways. Stick with it for the long haul until you reach the level of mastery they call "unconscious competence".
- Eventually, you may be able to capture in a simple, memorable formula the practice you've mastered to render harmless those longstanding triggers. It can go something like this:

When X … Then Y …

- For example, When X (my colleague challenges my thinking during our team meeting), Then Y (I will take a breath and respond calmly without becoming defensive, yet while also holding my ground)

Common Triggers Checklist

Here's a list of situations that often provoke an immediate physiological and emotional reaction in leaders. Which of these are triggers for you? See if you can identify your top 2-3.

______ Requests or demands that are issued without an appreciation of what's already on your plate
______ A colleague who frequently disagrees with you in a disagreeable way
______ Being left out of the loop on important emails or meetings
______ People not showing up to meetings on time
______ Being disrespected by your peers or boss in front of others
______ Having your credibility or expertise questioned
______ Being interrupted repeatedly
______ Email communication that discusses sensitive matters that would be better handled in person
______ Someone taking credit for others' work or failing to acknowledge the work of others
______ When someone misses a deadline to which he or she had agreed without notifying you in advance
______ Not being acknowledged for a job well done
______ When people bring you their problems without a proposed solution
______ Meetings that go on and on with no clear agenda or agreements made

*Source: *Missing Conversations: 9 Questions All Leaders Should Ask Themselves* by Bridgette Theurer & Heather Jelks, (2015)

Leadership Default Styles

All of us have a variety of ways that we exercise leadership---both at home and at work—and we routinely adjust our leadership style in light of what the overall situation requires. Parents instinctively know that they need to guide their teenager's behavior one way when s/he is navigating familiar social situations and in quite another way when the teen is experiencing the powerful emotions of a strongly conflictual relationship with a "best friend" for the first time. Workplace leaders routinely adjust their guidance of a new team facing a highly stressful challenge in one way, compared to how they lead a team of mature, self-directed workers who are following a well-established routine.

For the most part, we make the appropriate adjustments to our leadership style instinctively, without needing to give it much thought. But sometimes—and especially when facing highly stressful challenges—it is important for us to be more intentional about how best to lead in the midst of a highly anxious situation. Knowing which leadership style to choose in such situations can be complicated by the fact that all of us have certain ways of leading that feel more "natural" and comfortable to us. The problem is that sometimes those default styles may not be the best choice, particularly when the stress of the situation is infectious, and the "best choice" may not be immediately obvious.

When to use this tool:
Ideally, you will familiarize yourself with this tool before finding yourself in the midst of a situation that has triggered your reactivity. Reflecting on your default leadership style will probably be easier when you are not stressed out and need to take quick action. But even if the challenge is already upon you, spending some thoughtful time using this tool can help you make a better choice and—especially—may help you to avoid adopting a style that makes it even more difficult for those you lead to

manage themselves and the challenging situation they are facing. Becoming more self-aware will enable you to course-correct more quickly when you find yourself slipping into a leadership style that is not serving you or your team well.

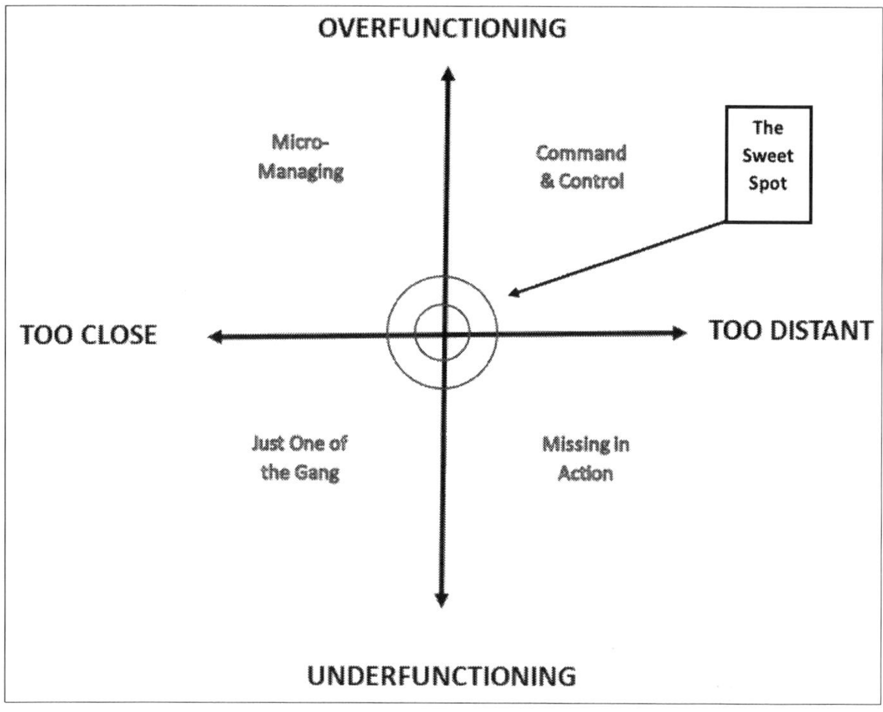

How to use this tool:

1. The Four Quadrants Diagram is built upon the content in Chapters 4 (Stay Connected) and Chapter 5 (Balance the See-Saw) in this book. Here is a quick summary of the two polarities that comprise each axis:
    - Overfunctioning means to "think, feel or act for another in a way that erodes the other's capacity for ownership." Feeling overly responsible, trying to solve other peoples' relationship dilemmas, or thinking you always know best are common examples of overfunctioning.

- Underfunctioning leaders allow their own anxieties, or the behavior of others, to diminish their functioning. Not speaking up, asking for advice too often, or failing to act out of fear about how others will react are examples of underfunctioning.
- Too Close: The healthy balance leaders must strike is to be "close enough to influence, but distant enough to lead." When leaders are too close to those they are leading they become emotionally enmeshed with them, compromise their ability to stand apart from the crowd, and lose their capacity for independent thought and action.
- Too Distant refers to a lack of connection, either with specific individuals a leader is managing or with the system as a whole. Leaders who are too distant may be perceived as aloof, uncaring, detached, or simply checked out. Such leaders lose their ability to influence the system positively.

2. On each axis, think about which direction you tend to move in when you are under stress. Is your default tendency to overfunction or underfunction? And do you instinctively move closer or withdraw when anxiety is high? Because these styles describe automatic functioning (rather than something that a leader consciously chooses) it may be challenging at first to see yourself in any of these quadrants. If this is the case, it might be helpful to ask yourself which of the four styles you think your team might pick if they were asked which quadrant best represents your default style. You may want to get help by discussing this tool with a coach, mentor, or trusted friend. Sometimes your spouse can act as a resource as well, especially in recognizing

your leadership style at home, which may be different from your dominant style at work.

Sometimes it is easier to start out by thinking of the default style of others. How does your boss operate under pressure, and how does this impact others in the workplace? Are there any leaders in your organization whose default style under stress is crystal clear to you? Remember, each of the four styles is a coping strategy for managing anxiety. You may even be able to recognize certain conditions that raise anxiety (for you or others) and trace the reactivity that results in the cluster of behaviors that characterize one of the four quadrants. [For example: "Every time our revenue numbers are falling short as we approach the end of the quarter, John goes into Command & Control mode, while Phyllis is Missing in Action."] As we get more skilled in recognizing certain default leadership styles in others, we often grow our skill of recognizing those same automatic patterns in us!

Reflecting on how you behave in specific situations may help you become more self-aware of the innate tendencies that show up in you when you are stressed. But even if you're not able to identify with certainty where you tend to go while under stress, you can be certain that you—like all of us—will visit both ends of each axis on occasion. For that reason, it is valuable to study the leadership style of all four quadrants. Spend time studying each description below and try to recall when you may have exhibited some of the behaviors described. In this way you should get a deeper sense of what each default leadership style looks like in action.

Micro-Managing

What It Looks Like:

- Inserts self in the details of others' work when it's not warranted
- Often corrects and/or does the work of others
- Asks too often for updates on "where do things stand?"
- Overly prescriptive on how things should be done

How It Impacts Leaders and Others:

- Time spent "in the weeds" distracts leaders from higher-level strategic issues
- The leader becomes the "bottleneck" that holds things up
- The team feels resentful and becomes less productive
- Burnout (in leaders and others) becomes more likely
- Leader's anxiety keeps escalating from the vain effort to manage "everything"

Command & Control

What It Looks Like:

- Tells others what to do and/or how they should think or feel
- Struggles to share power with others
- Delegates responsibility but not authority
- Makes decisions without prior consultation or input from others
- Discourages dissent

How It Impacts Leaders and Others:

- Weakens others' sense of ownership
- Stifles creativity, risk-taking, and innovation
- Others stop thinking for themselves

- Results in poor decisions (since those closest to the process have not been consulted)
- Invites resistance and sabotage (because others don't feel they have a voice in decisions that impact them)

Missing-in-Action

What It Looks Like:

- Withdraws or retreats, emotionally or physically, or both
- Lacks presence and visibility
- Allows decisions or issues to fester too long before addressing them
- Fails to hold others accountable
- Does not speak up with conviction in key conversations

How it Impacts Leaders and Others:

- Creates a leadership vacuum that raises the anxiety of followers
- Team dynamics become more reactive and less aligned
- Lack of clarity and communication slows decision-making and often results in do-overs
- Loss of influence (You can't influence a system you are not connected to.)

Just One of the Gang

What It Looks Like:

- Errs on the side of being a friend versus being a boss
- Worries about being liked, making everyone happy
- Avoids conflict and confrontation
- Fails to enforce clear boundaries

How it Impacts Leaders and Others:

- Leader loses credibility
- Leaders easily swept up in the emotional highs and lows of others
- High performers frustrated at leader's failure to confront under-performers
- Team performance is eroded

Dealing with Resistance

When we "think systems," resistance that may initially appear to be perverse or even intentional sabotage can be understood as a "natural" response of a system to a perceived threat. It is in the very nature of a system to resist threats to its integrity, to "push back" so as not to lose the finely tuned balance that has allowed it to thrive up to this point. This instinct to "self-correct" is an attempt to regain the familiar, comfortable status quo of the system ("But we've always done it this way!"). Recognizing the power of this force of nature that can literally feel like it is about survival helps us to understand and deal with resistance from a more thoughtful, rather than reactive, stance. Here are some "Best Practices" that represent thoughtful ways of dealing with resistance:

1. **Expect It.** This is what systems do in the face of change. Remember that it's not about you, even when it's directed at you. Don't take it personally!

2. **Distinguish between reactive and productive complaints.** Beware of being caught up in contagious reactivity or spending too much time formulating logical arguments to "convince" the opposition. (Mindless sabotage is impervious to reason!). On the other hand, productive complaints (thoughtful resistance) are open to reasonable self-interest and will usually respond when your explanations minimize perceived threats and maximize the rewards associated with change. (cf. David Rock's SCARF model)

   SCARF Acronym defined:
   - Status – our relative importance to others.
   - Certainty – our ability to predict the future.
   - Autonomy – our sense of control over events.

- Relatedness – how safe we feel with others.
- Fairness – how fair we perceive the exchanges between people to be.

3. **Stay connected to those who resist your leadership efforts.** Resist the temptation to distance yourself and instead, stay connected in a non-anxious way. You can only influence a system to which you are connected—the same goes with people.

4. **Take good care of yourself (physically and emotionally).** This will give you the stamina you need to persevere. Reactive sabotage can be single-minded, relentless, and seemingly inexhaustible. You will need what it takes to stick with it over the long haul.

5. **Remain playful and use humor as a way to lower your own and others' anxiety** (be a step-down transformer). Humor will keep you from being "hijacked" by others' reactive intensity better than anything. It also helps you to keep the big-picture perspective in the "fog of war".

6. **Don't allow others' anxious behavior to sidetrack you**. Remember that seemingly unrelated phenomena that negatively impact a change initiative are often disguised forms of anxiety-driven reactivity (e.g., forgetfulness, increased levels of mistakes, absenteeism, and accidents, escalating gossiping and blaming, and internal conflict). In the face of these various forms of resistance—both overt and covert—a resilient leader's best course of action will be to keep focused on his/her own functioning and not be "sidetracked" by distractions.

7. **Allow some opportunity for venting, while keeping people focused on the future.** ("You can let people visit pity city, but don't let them park there!") Whenever possible respond to productive complaints by accommodating reasonable suggestions.

8. **Don't inadvertently invite resistance.** Minimize sabotage and resistance by avoiding obvious triggers to reactivity. Don't push the "hot buttons" needlessly.

9. **Help people to see the opportunities that change opens up for them.** Look for ways to harness reactive energies by turning them into adaptive behaviors—part of an evolutionary process that naturally will seek the safety of a "new normal".

Getting on the Balcony

Definition:

Observing yourself, others, and your system with curiosity in order to build self-awareness and expand your capacity for thoughtful action

How it Works:

- **Hit the pause button and step back** (and up) to broaden your perspective. Take a few mindful breaths to calm your nervous system.
- **Get curious:** Ask questions to gain insight into the reactivity you see in yourself, others, or the system. One question you might ask from the balcony is, "What's really going on here?"
- **Choose a thoughtful response:** Decide from the balcony what response from you will be most effective in terms of lessening reactivity (in yourself or others) and moving things forward in a productive way.

A Few Examples:

- Your teenager's hostile attitude pushes your buttons and evokes a reactive response from you that only serves to make things worse. You're surprised at yourself and later you're curious about what is going on in the larger family system that might have made your fuse so short in the exchange with him.

- Your boss is distant, curt, and sends defensive emails that make you anxious. Rather than react, you become curious and think about what stresses he's dealing with in the larger organizational system he's part of as a senior leader.

- You've worked with your team to become more thoughtful when situations escalate the pressure on them to "do more with less". But in a meeting you watch as a new set of demands triggers intense reactivity within the group. You intervene quickly by asking them questions that require them to explore the situation from a broader perspective.

Leading Your Team "From the Balcony"

When to use:

Whenever your team is having a breakdown with another team or is at an impasse in some way, help them to get on the balcony so that they can *think their way through their dilemma,* rather than simply react to it.

How to use:

1. Gather your team and introduce the meaning of "getting on the balcony" (i.e., stepping back and up to broaden our perspective, bringing an attitude of curiosity & openness, and observing ourselves and others with discernment versus judgment).

2. Frame the situation or challenge and invite them to focus on it with curiosity.

3. Engage in a dialogue of inquiry using the following questions as a guide:
    a. What are the facts here and how do we know?
    b. What assumptions are we making about this situation?
    c. What is going on in the larger system—specifically, are levels of stress and anxiety on the rise? If so, what are the sources of that stress and anxiety?

d. How are people reacting to those stressors?

e. How are *we* reacting? Which of our behaviors are helping to move things forward and which might be hindering progress?

f. What are our best ideas for moving forward in a new way?

4. Identify a thoughtful response the team can make. The exact nature of this response can only be determined from the balcony, but possible actions may include:

   a. Identifying the "Missing Conversation" that needs to take place and engaging in it from a calm and clear place – Who needs to be brought together to discuss what?

   b. Reframing the situation so that both parties can engage from a more open and less defensive place.

   c. Clarifying roles, responsibilities or processes, and building shared understanding and alignment around them.

GLOSSARY OF TERMS

Acute anxiety: A transient state of unease in the face of a current threat. Acute anxiety is a temporary psychological and physiological state of heightened stress that is provoked by an immediate situation or set of circumstances that are perceived as threatening. People can be and generally are consciously aware of being in such a state.

Chronic anxiety: An abiding sense of unease about imagined or anticipated threats. Chronic anxiety is present to some degree in all human systems and typically lies beneath the conscious awareness of its members. Key sources of chronic anxiety are threats to five primal human needs: control, safety, approval, belonging, and certainty.

Cutoff and Fusion: Default tendencies developed as a way to handle the stress and anxiety in relationship systems. A *cutoff* happens when a person moves toward extreme distance (emotionally or physically) to such a degree that there is no longer a connection with a person (or group) who are emotionally significant. *Fusion* happens when a person becomes so emotionally entangled and reactive with another person (or group) that it is no longer possible to tell where self ends and the other begins.

Differentiation of self: An individual's capacity for independent thought and action (self-definition) while maintaining a balanced connection to significant others (self-regulation).

Emotional system: The emotional system is composed of the instinctive pattern of automatic actions, reactions, and interactions that shape the functioning of an individual, team, organization, or any network of relationships.

Fallacy of empathy: The mistaken belief that offering support, understanding, and comfort to others (especially to those who are poorly differentiated) will, by itself, promote in them greater responsibility for self.

Immune system: Based on the analogy of how the body's immune system works, the image of the leader as immune system suggests the importance of leaders increasing the resilience of an organization by providing challenges that increase the members' ability to tolerate pain and persist in the face of difficulties.

Lead with conviction: To act boldly, take clear stands, and be willing to take risks (even when it makes you vulnerable to failure and ridicule) for the sake of preserving core values or creating a new future you care about.

Less anxious presence: An ability to embody and communicate inner calm in a way that helps others lower their own anxiety.

New Way of LEADING: The exercise of leadership by focusing first on one's own self-differentiation, *staying connected* to others in a balanced and healthy way, and *leading with conviction* by functioning in a less reactive, more thoughtful, and principled fashion.

New Way of SEEING: The ability of a leader to recognize the presence and influence of automatic, reactive patterns in self, others, and the relationship systems of which the leader is a part.

New Way of THINKING: The ability of a leader to "think systems" by reflecting thoughtfully on the actions, reactions, and interactions that s/he has observed among people in the emotional system of which the leader is a part. In thinking systems, a leader understands situations and behaviors in light of certain universal, basic principles of how all emotional systems operate.

Overfunctioning: To think, feel, or act for another in a way that erodes their own capacity for ownership or thoughtful action. Whenever a leader is overfunctioning, there is a reciprocal underfunctioning response somewhere else in the system.

Presence of the past: In emotional systems (families or organizations), inherited, automatic patterns of behavior are passed down from one generation to another, usually with no recognition as to their origin or their continuing influence on current behavior.

Reactivity: The automatic response of an organism to a perceived threat. Reactivity is the public face of anxiety.

Self-differentiating move: An action or position a leader takes that charts a new course for the leader and the leader's team/organization and is based on thoughtful consideration of the leader's vision, values, and guiding principles.

Stay connected: The ability to strike a healthy balance with stakeholders by being "close enough to influence yet distant enough to lead."

Step-down transformer: Based on how an electrical transformer works, the metaphor suggests the important role that a leader plays in an organization by staying connected as a less anxious presence, thus helping to calm the system and make it more thoughtful, more efficient, and more productive.

Triangle: A triad between three people (or two people and an unresolved issue or conflict) that is formed to lower the stress being experienced between two of the people. Triangles are universal and can be either healthy or toxic, depending on a person's position in them and how the person functions within them.

Underfunctioning: Allowing the behavior of others to diminish one's own functioning.

Made in the USA
Columbia, SC
26 June 2024